On African-American

MW00652589

On African-American Rhetoric traces the arc of strategic language use by African Americans from rhetorical forms such as slave narratives and the spirituals to Black digital expression and contemporary activism. The governing idea is to illustrate the basic call-response process of African-American culture and to demonstrate how this dynamic has been and continues to be central to the language used by African Americans to make collective cultural and political statements. Ranging across genres and disciplines, including rhetorical theory, poetry, fiction, folklore, speeches, music, film, pedagogy, and memes, Gilyard and Banks consider language developments that have occurred both inside and outside of organizations and institutions. Along with paying attention to recent events, this book incorporates discussion of important forerunners who have carried the rhetorical baton. These include Frederick Douglass, Harriet Jacobs, Sojourner Truth, Anna Julia Cooper, W.E.B. Du Bois, Zora Neale Hurston, Malcolm X, Martin Luther King, Jr., Toni Cade Bambara, Molefi Asante, Alice Walker, and Geneva Smitherman. Written for students and professionals alike, this book is powerful and instructive regarding the long African-American quest for freedom and dignity.

Keith Gilyard works at The Pennsylvania State University, where he is the Edwin Erle Sparks Professor of English and African-American Studies and Senior Faculty Mentor in the Office of Educational Equity. His books include *Voices of the Self: A Study of Language Competence* (1991) and *True to the Language Game: African American Discourse, Cultural Politics, and Pedagogy* (2011).

Adam J. Banks is Professor and Faculty Director, Program in Writing and Rhetoric at Stanford University. Previous books include *Race, Rhetoric, and Technology: Searching for Higher Ground* (2006) and *Digital Griots: African American Rhetoric in a Multimedia Age* (2011).

On African-American Rhetoric

Keith Gilyard and Adam J. Banks

Routledge
Taylor & Francis Group

NEW YORK AND LONDON

First published 2018
by Routledge
711 Third Avenue, New York, NY 10017

and by Routledge
2 Park Square, Milton Park, Abingdon, Oxon OX14 4RN

Routledge is an imprint of the Taylor & Francis Group, an informa business

© 2018 Taylor & Francis

The right of Keith Gilyard and Adam J. Banks to be identified as the authors of this work has been asserted by them in accordance with sections 77 and 78 of the Copyright, Designs and Patents Act 1988.

All rights reserved. No part of this book may be reprinted or reproduced or utilised in any form or by any electronic, mechanical, or other means, now known or hereafter invented, including photocopying and recording, or in any information storage or retrieval system, without permission in writing from the publishers.

Trademark notice: Product or corporate names may be trademarks or registered trademarks, and are used only for identification and explanation without intent to infringe.

Library of Congress Cataloging-in-Publication Data
Names: Gilyard, Keith, 1952- author. | Banks, Adam J. (Adam Joel)
Title: On African–American rhetoric / Keith Gilyard and Adam J. Banks.
Description: New York, NY : Routledge, 2018. | Includes bibliographical
    references.
Identifiers: LCCN 2017050669 | ISBN 9781138090422 (hardcover) | ISBN
    9781138090446 (softcover) | ISBN 9781315108636 (ebook)
Subjects: LCSH: African Americans—Communication. | African
    Americans—Intellectual life. | African Americans in popular culture. |
    Black English—Rhetoric. | Oratory—United States. | Black English.
Classification: LCC P94.5.A37 G45 2018 | DDC 427/.973—dc23
LC record available at https://lccn.loc.gov/2017050669

ISBN: 978-1-138-09042-2 (hbk)
ISBN: 978-1-138-09044-6 (pbk)
ISBN: 978-1-315-10863-6 (ebk)

Typeset in Goudy
by Apex CoVantage, LLC

For the students, teachers, scholars, and everyday folk
by whom the tradition lives

Contents

Acknowledgments

We express deep gratitude to our editor, Nicole Solano, and her colleagues at Routledge for embracing the promise of the project and helping to bring it to fruition. We thank three anonymous reviewers along with David Green and Earl Brooks for their encouragement and for comments that strengthened the manuscript. Lastly, we recognize our wonderful research assistants, Mudiwa Pettus and Brandon Erby. They also provided constructive feedback and handled many of the details of manuscript preparation.

1 Introduction

"We look at Miss Moore and she lookin at us, waiting for I dunno what" (92). Sylvia, the headstrong narrator of Toni Cade Bambara's dexterous 1960s-era short story "The Lesson," sums up a predicament at F.A.O. Schwarz, the high-end toy store in ritzy midtown Manhattan to which she and seven other Harlem children have been escorted on a summertime field trip by a benevolent neighbor. Amid the stunning show of privilege, dramatized most starkly by a toy sailboat in the display window bearing a price tag of $1,195, the children begin consciously to consider wealth disparity in the United States and how economic imbalance is mapped onto ethnicities. Contemplating the sailboat, Sylvia thinks, "For some reason this pisses me off" (92). It is at this point that she and the other children—her cousin Sugar, Flyboy, Fat Butt, Junebug, Q.T., Rosie Giraffe, and Mercedes—exchange looks with their guide, who nudges them into the store for further exploration. Once inside, the usually confident Sylvia becomes shy, experiences shame, and then becomes enraged. As Sugar runs a finger over the sailboat, Sylvia muses, "And I'm jealous and want to hit her. Maybe not her, but I sure want to punch somebody in the mouth" (94). Although she generally avoids conversing directly with Miss Moore, because she does not want to validate fully Moore's educational project, she asks why she and the others had been brought to the store. Miss Moore declines to answer, replying instead, "You sound angry, Sylvia. Are you mad about something?" (94). Sylvia refuses to give the satisfaction of an answer, moping around the store instead until she convinces the other children to call a halt to the adventure.

On the subway ride back uptown, our protagonist ponders the lives of people who can afford the extravagance exhibited in midtown: "What kinda work they do and how they live and how come we ain't in on it?" (94). She is mainly ignorant concerning the larger world but has become conscious that she needs to learn a lot more about how it operates. Most important, and this is the realization animating her by the end of the story, her crucial issue is to figure out how not to let that world suppress her and leave her behind.

Although Sylvia would have to wait years to be able to understand the matter in sophisticated terms, she and the other children are steeped in the discourse of a racist and capitalist system. In fact, most of Harlem is. This system promotes economic winners and losers and ensures that Black people lose at a disproportionate rate. But the system does even more than this. It thrives on and supports language that makes all of the winning and losing seem normal and even fair. So the children supposedly are in their proper place as well as thinking and acting as waywardly and, ultimately, as subserviently as they should. Books convey the message of inferiority. Myths. Television. Movies. This language structures thought, and children can only transcend it through intervention. Indeed, the aptly named Miss Moore performs the nec-essary action. She brings *moore* or, spelled conventionally, *more* information. By gathering the children outside of school, outside of the official channels of communication, as well as outside of their comfortable spatial-linguistic environs, she provides generative contrast.

Moore/more information constitutes an *epistemic break*. For theorist and rhetorician Michel Foucault (1969/1972), *epistemes* were concepts that counted as legitimate knowledge, and they were circulated and reproduced by means of related and regulated discursive practices (pp. 191–2).[1] Sylvia is governed by a discourse that spurs and justifies her ignorance, and, as such, she initially resists the interruption of Miss Moore, whom she quite unorig-inally reduces to a "nappy-head bitch and her goddamn college degree" ("The Lesson," p. 88). In her mind, she equates her would-be mentor to the annoying winos who piss up the parks and hallways of the neighborhood. Nonetheless, Miss Moore, aided by the guardians who entrust their children to her, begins to orchestrate the break. Her lectures have little effect, as Sylvia reveals at the outset of the trip: "So we heading down the street and she's boring us silly about what things cost and what our parents make and how much goes for rent and how money ain't divided up right in this country" (p. 89). She would rather think about meeting some cute boys. But Miss Moore, in the manner of the great educator Paulo Freire (1970), comprehends that the teacher-dominant, overly narrative approach is inef-ficient and relatively ineffective.[2] The children need not another sermon from an adult. They need field experience. Sylvia, for example, whose name literally means "one who lives in the woods," her forest being not so much Harlem but her state of mind, has to be led physically to greater awareness. The break will be complete when she and the other children merge *moore/ more information* with the felt sense of their excursion and exclusion as they fashion a counter narrative.

Back in the neighborhood at the mailbox (where messages are sent), which is the site from which the trip originated, we witness some of the results of Miss Moore's efforts. The pressure gets to Sylvia during the debriefing; she "got a headache for thinkin so hard" (p. 95). To her disliking, her cousin is fully atten-tive, sounding like a little Miss Moore and offering the astute remarks, "I think that this is not much of a democracy if you ask me. Equal chance to pursue happiness means an equal crack at the dough, don't it?" (p. 95). Miss Moore then fixes her gaze on Sylvia, who feels that something "weird" is transpiring, palpable in her chest (p. 95). Still somewhat defiant, she will not contribute when Miss Moore asks if anyone besides Sugar has learned anything that day. Instead she storms off and seeks solitude.

Understandings no longer align easily for Sylvia. Concepts do not match perceptions. Matters are incongruous, which, ironically, is the key to her development. According to Kenneth Burke (1984), perspective by incongruity occurs when "a word belongs by custom to a certain category—and by rational planning you wrench it loose and metaphorically apply it to a different category. . . . It is designed to 'remoralize' by accurately naming a situation already demoralized by inaccuracy" (pp. 308–9). *Justice,* for example, as Sylvia will come to know, cannot be attached to a system in which toy sailboats for some cost more than the combined monthly rent paid by the families of Ms. Moore's charges. The word *justice* has to be detached from oppressive arrangements and, in Burke's parlance, remoralized. The term cannot sanction capitalism, racism, and their manifestations. Nor can *democracy,* as Sugar knows. By extension, as Miss Moore has already discerned, an entire discourse of opportunity and uplift has to be remoralized if it is to serve the purpose of Black liberation. Alternative viewpoints are no guarantee that an exploitative social order will be replaced, but no such societal arrangement can, in fact, be achieved without alternative viewpoints. Sylvia ultimately promises to embody fresh perspectives as she sheds part of her old identity. Miss Moore, although surely cognizant of the psychic pain that could accompany Sylvia's growth, does not want it any other way.

Moore/more information illustrates the fundamental nature of African-American rhetoric, which for present purposes is defined as the art of persuasion fused with African-American ways of knowing in attempts to achieve in public realms personhood, dignity, and respect, as scholar Deborah Atwater (2009) put it, for African-American people (p. 1). Of course, this definition is elastic but not exhaustive. No specific political perspective predominates, and much strategic verbal behavior occurs in private, interpersonal contexts and in broad displays of play and entertainment. But from old exhortations to New World Africans that, in essence, their lives were Black to recent declarations that Black lives matter, a major strand of African-American appeal has aimed to persuade American society to live up to its expressed ideals about equality and rights. Books, journals, audiovisual materials, and digital archives contain vast storehouses of essays, speeches, and artistic performances as well as related analyses. We no doubt are interested in all of these artifacts. Notwithstanding, our focused interest currently is on a sampling of how African-American rhetors have consciously employed African-American rhetoric as a critical method, in other words, how they have demonstrated meta-awareness that the tropes and texts emergent from African-American culture and integral to it comprise a usable code. However, by *code* we do not mean a body of rules established only by academic or scholarly theorists. As Jennifer Richards (2008) notes, "we might also describe as 'rhetorical' those writings which are not informed by formal training in rhetoric, but which engage their readers in a process of deliberation on different sides" (14). Conceived this way,

African-American rhetoric is as much about trading in story as it is about the application of schemata.

In 1926, in the decade before Bambara's birth, W.E.B. Du Bois opined famously in "Criteria of Negro Art" that, "despite the wailing of purists," he rejected the notion of art-for-art's sake and considered all art to be politically instrumental (p. 296.) He added, "I stand in utter shamelessness and say that whatever art I have for writing has been used always for propaganda for gaining the right of black folk to love and enjoy. I do not care a damn for any art that is not used for propaganda" (p. 296). Bambara, who would co-author a script for a documentary about Du Bois,[3] fulfills his prescription in "The Lesson," a story instructive for her ideal audience. As are the characters in the story, we readers are asked to consider which discourses are hegemonic and why. Moreover, Bambara pushes us to contest some of those discourses as she did as an author and activist, and she points to Black possibility. The story reveals the essential beauty of the "black as hell" Miss Moore (p. 87). It shows that African-American youth in urban communities are reachable and teachable if there is collective will to do so and we consider them to be valuable members of the community. The children's parents, although they talk behind Miss Moore's back "like a dog," contribute mightily (pp. 87–8). They not only make the kids presentable, they in fact *present* them to Miss Moore. The implied question is whether there will always be enough Miss Moores available to receive them.

Du Bois had hinted at this problem in "Of the Coming of John," the only fiction selection in *The Souls of Black Folk* (1903/1994). The character John Jones, forerunner to both Sylvia and Miss Moore, experiences an epiphany on completing his education at Wells Institute:

> He looked now for the first time sharply about him, and wondered he had seen so little before. He grew slowly to feel almost for the first time the Veil[4] that lay between him and the white world; he first noticed now the oppression that had not seemed oppression before, differences that erstwhile seemed natural, restraints and slights that in his boyhood days had gone unnoticed or been greeted with a laugh. He felt angry now when men did not call him "Mister," he clenched his hands at the "Jim Crow" cars and chafed at the color-line that hemmed in him and his. A tinge of sarcasm crept into his speech, and a vague bitterness into his life; and he sat long hours wondering and planning a way around these crooked things.
>
> (pp. 144–5)

After graduation, John eventually returns after an absence of seven years to the segregated town of Altamaha, Georgia, where he resolves to impact the community by teaching at the Negro school. To undertake this task he must seek the permission of town patriarch Judge Henderson, who has no use for liberal ideas when it comes to African Americans. As Henderson interrogates, "Now, John, the question is, are you, with your education and Northern notions, going to accept the situation and teach the darkies to be faithful servants and laborers as your fathers were" (p. 150). The judge informs John that he knew his father, who had belonged to the judge's brother and was a "good Nigger" (p. 150). Then he rephrases and presses home the central question: "Well, are you going to be like him, or are you going to try to put fool ideas of rising and equality into these folks' heads, and make them discontented and unhappy?" (p. 150).

John agrees to accept the status quo but cannot abide by the decision because the epistemic break that he has experienced at Wells Institute has been too profound. His cold seriousness has replaced the jovial demeanor of years past, and he hardly fits in among the African Americans of Altamaha. Yet he fully accepts the consequences of his education, as he conveys to his sister Jennie:

> "John," she said, "does it make every one—unhappy when they study and learn lots of things?"
>
> He paused and smiled. "I'm afraid it does," he said.
>
> "And, John, are you glad you studied?"
>
> "Yes," came the answer, slowly but positively.
>
> (p. 149)

John shares with his students some of the lessons that he has learned, including ideas about social equality and matters such as the French Revolution. Later, after complaints by the some of the town's White citizens that John failed to conform to expectations, Henderson closes the school. John's life immediately takes a disastrous turn when, defending his sister from being sexually assaulted, he kills Henderson's son and is hunted in return. He becomes a tragic torchbearer in the struggle to combat ignorance and maintain dignity.

John is resurrected in Bambara's hands. Moreover, she not only created Miss Moore in art, she publicly embraced the role of artist as instructor. For example, before lectures and readings, Bambara often used her dialogue "The Golden Bandit," a revision of "Goldilocks and the Three Bears," to remind people to scrutinize official versions and authorized tales ("Golden Bandit," 1995, p. 207). The narrator and interlocutors conclude their exchange about that "burglar-chile-vandal-thief," who will not confess to her exploits or take responsibility for them, choosing instead to frame the bears":

> Did she elicit the help of her parents, presumably grown-ups, presumably grown and capable of analyzing the normative values of their tribe/community/household that have given rise to the sociopathic behavior of their little warped offspring—in short, Good People, did this retrograde little heifer seize the time and engage in principled self-criticism?
>
> None of that, naw.
>
> She said some bears were chasing her.
>
> A liar on top of everything else.

Well, err, rahhh, I heard tell that this little yellow-haired gal was a child-hood hero of yours.

No way. Puhleeze. I'll admit it, but I was young and foolish at the time.

Well, then, do you think it is hip, healthy, or wise to inflict little children with the official version of the golden bandit before we have assumed the necessary task of encouraging and equipping the young in a critical habit?

No, no, no.

A critical habit is crucial, wouldn't you say, afflicted as we are every day with err, rahhh . . .

Authorized versions. Lies. Cover-ups. Disinformation.

Are you saying, Good People, that an official text is often a con text?

Got that right.

That's exactly what the three convicted bears and their lawyer claimed on appeal. The end.

(pp. 209–10)

And with her narrator's summation, Bambara cemented her legacy as an important figure, as is Du Bois, in African-American rhetoric studies.

On African-American Rhetoric continues to trace the arc of strategic language use by African Americans as incorporated in rhetorical forms such as slave narratives, the spirituals, poetry, fiction, folklore, speeches, music, film, and memes. A principal idea is to illustrate the basic call-response process (Du Bois-Bambara) of African-American communities and to demonstrate how this dynamic has been and continues to be central to the language used by African Americans to make individual and collective statements about politics and culture. This book is not a definitive presentation; the field is too large and varied to accomplish that in one project. No volume could fully account for the range of aims, audiences, arguments, appeals, and aesthetics that we find in even a single day of Black rhetorical production, especially in this era of information overload. Any study could only itself be a call that hopes for response. So, as indicated, we have collected representative anecdotes and texts to describe the critical and methodical nature of the African-American rhetorical tradition—*rhetorical* because it is a body of work that in its self-reflection stresses the various sides of issues and a *tradition* because it is held together even in all of its variety by particular textual maneuvers.

Amiri Baraka's notion of the "changing same" is instructive. He coined the term in 1966 to name the dialectic between jazz and racist oppression, observing that the music evolved stylistically while always managing to challenge shifting forms of domination (1966/1991, pp. 203–9). Or as Erik Mortenson (2010) explains,

What changes is both the means by which oppression does its work as well as the form of the response that African American music takes to address that oppression. What remains the same is both the continual assault on African American freedom in the form of racism as well as the consistent attitude of rebellion in the face of such assault.

(p. 68)

Baraka's "changing same" keeps us attuned to history and to social context. For example, Black Twitter demonstrates a "changing same" in African-American rhetoric: built on modes of discourse and persuasive strategies rooted in African-American oral traditions and yet constantly shifting more quickly than software and updated passwords. It operates within fissures of history, ideas, and technologies, and it creates further ruptures or breaks.

But first a closer look at those roots. Chapter 2 highlights some of the major achievements of African-American rhetors over the course of American history, including the creation of the slave narrative, the verbal constitution of a group known as "African Americans," and the formation of a musical tradition rooted in the spirituals and the blues. All of these rhetorical forms remain stirring articulations of Black yearnings and eloquent arguments for Black humanity. Individuals discussed include Olaudah Equiano, David Walker, Frederick Douglass, Harriet Jacobs, and Malcolm X. Moreover, it is worth pointing out that African Americans on the whole always have understood rhetorical and/or literate practices to be competitive arenas and have relished the opportunities to participate in them. Not much time in the tradition has been spent in contemplative angst about philosophy-rhetoric splits of the kind indicated by Plato in *Gorgias* (c. 387 BCE)—the philosopher seeking Truth and the rhetorician seeking to win an argument at any cost (p. 247). Nor have African-American scholars seriously questioned the value of rhetoric. They have not been bogged down in questions of whether rhetoric is merely spin or specious talk or an art or indeterminate linguistic practice or a repressive system or even dead (as in eclipsed by scientific reasoning).[5] The focus has been on the quest for freedom and on those who have struggled for freedom—as well as sought "small t" truths—with the tool of rhetoric.

Chapter 3 addresses the major pendulum swing of African-American rhetoric. Harold Cruse noted in *The Crisis of the Negro Intellectual* that African Americans have always oscillated between the integrationist strain and the separatist strain, a tension that some refer to as the push-pull dynamic of African-American culture ((1967/1984, pp. 4–6). The most celebrated rhetorical expression of the integrationist strain has been through the African-American jeremiad, whose celebrated practitioners have included David Walker, Frederick Douglass, W.E.B Du Bois, Mary McLeod Bethune, Martin Luther King, Jr., and Michelle Alexander. Notable separatist arguments have been made by Du Bois (because the oscillation is very real), Marcus Garvey, Elijah Muhammad, and Malcolm X. Using as a starting point Sutton Griggs's *Imperio in Imperium*

(1899/2003), perhaps the classic "rhetoric novel" in the African-American literary tradition, one that incorporates both integrationist and separatist impulses, we map the push-pull of African-American rhetoric from the nineteenth century to contemporary times.

In the subsequent chapter, we consider the prominent theories of African-American rhetoric that circulate in American colleges and university courses. These include the ideas of Molefi Kete Asante, perhaps the field's foremost theoretician, as evident by his books *Rhetoric of Black Revolution* (1969); *The Afrocentric Idea* (1998); and *Race, Rhetoric, and Identity* (2005). Also addressed are the constructs proffered by Henry Louis Gates, Jr. in *Figures in Black* (1987) and *The Signifying Monkey* (1988a). Gates describes his work as such: "my movement, then, is from hermeneutics to rhetoric and semantics, only to return to hermeneutics once again" (*Signifying Monkey*, p. 44). We are concerned primarily with the rhetoric phase of the journey. The latter third of the chapter speaks to the cluster of ideologies that we term, for convenience, *Black feminism*, notions that cohere around four tropes: 1) the self-conscious verbal assertion of requisite Black female presence, 2) commentary about the exercise of a Black female voice speaking against male domination, 3) the ironic assertion of high-achieving Black womanhood, and 4) the positing of triple exploitation. Writings by Anna Julia Cooper, Zora Neale Hurston, and Alice Walker will be featured in this section.

The relationship of technology to African-American rhetoric is the subject of Chapter 5. We consider a central question: How does Black rhetorical production respond to the tension between the possibilities for collective action, community building, and everyday expression that our increased reliance on technologies enables and the complicity of technologies in racialized systems of oppression? We view Stevie Wonder, who embraced electronic music in the period after gaining his artistic independence from Motown, as an exemplar because of his production, design, and advocacy in the face of the conflicts between oppression and agency.

Chapter 6 explores Black Twitter. While the phenomenon has received significant media attention ranging from genuine curiosity to lazy reporting, outright appropriation, and growing scholarly attention, very little of that attention has taken up the question of what rhetorical features allow it to operate as such a powerful and important space for Black community online. This chapter will explore those rhetorical features and functions as they operate not only in Black Twitter as a communal space but in this contemporary moment of activism.

Writing instruction has long been a central topic for rhetoric theorists, a fact symbolized by the labels *Rhet/Comp* and *Comp/Rhet*, which are common designators in American colleges and universities. Chapter 7 speaks to the historical presence of African-American instructors and scholars in the field of composition studies. Important forerunners include elocutionist, activist, and educator Hallie Quinn Brown and historian Carter G. Woodson. More recent figures to be considered include Geneva Smitherman, Kermit Campbell, and Carmen Kynard.

The concluding chapter involves both retrospect and prospect. Although African-American appeals to authenticity built on tradition remain important, we are living in an era in which tradition is subject to rigorous new critique. This closing reflection will make explicit the call that our book issues, identifying future directions for the study of African-American rhetoric and some of the voices, networks, movements, and spaces students and scholars might explore together. The ephemeral nature of overwhelmingly fast and voluminous digital communication means that we all need to be archivists; we all need to save, sample, and Storify. We all need to see curating our own Freedom's Mixtape as part of how we work through the complexities of rhetoric in the pursuit of life, love, and liberation, across all the convergences and differences that mark any community at any moment in time. Sylvia, fully mature, understands completely.

Notes

1. For more discussion of Foucault and epistemes, see Mills (*Discourse*, 2004, pp. 50–4.)
2. Freire considered education to be "suffering from narration sickness" because rigid and disabling relationships between teachers (narrating subjects) and students (patient, listening objects) (*Pedagogy of the Oppressed*, 1970, p. 57). The material narrated thus tends, according to Freire, to "become lifeless and petrified" (p. 57).
3. *W.E.B. Du Bois: A Biography in Four Voices*, directed by Louis Massiah (1997).
4. Du Bois uses the metaphor of the veil throughout *The Souls of Black Folk* to represent the distorted view that African Americans have as a result of racism. For an elaborate discussion, see Gibson ("Introduction," 1989, pp. xi–xv).
5. For an overview regarding these issues, see Richards (*Rhetoric*, 2008, pp. 3–12). Also see the extended sections "The Death of Rhetoric" (pp. 121–9) and "Post-Structural Rhetoric" (pp. 129–35).

2 Historical Overview of African-American Rhetoric

From the Greek *rhētorikē*, meaning the art of speaking, *rhetoric* as a particular body of work about strategic language use has a 2,500-year history in the West, although *rhetorical activity*, which we also generally refer to as *rhetoric*, is much older of course and more geographically dispersed. People have been using language strategically everywhere about as long as they have been strategizing and, if you will, languaging. Thus, rhetoric is more substantive and serious, and in many instances more honorable and worthy of study, than suggested in contemporary descriptions, particularly those in the media. Typically, when pundits ridicule articulations opposing theirs as *just rhetoric* or think that they are moving conversations forward by declaring *enough of the rhetoric*, they are really signaling that they privilege *their own dismissive rhetoric*. They are not operating outside of rhetorical behavior. At any rate, rhetoric has set in motion too many positive actions by African Americans for them to belittle the art categorically, or at least that should be the case.

It is not that African Americans require a complex Greek labeling system. There is no straight line from the ruminations of Aristotle to modern Black thought and verbal output. We incorporate figures and tropes into our culture without necessarily realizing their classical names. For example, it is doubtful that African-American songwriters Freddie Perren and Keni St. Lewis were influenced by the terms *syllogism* or *enthymeme* when they penned "Heaven Must Be Missing an Angel" for the singing group Tavares (1976). Yet we understand the logic of their artistic world:

1. Angels live in heaven. (implied major premise)
2. You are (an angel) here with me. (implied minor premise)
3. Therefore, heaven must be missing an angel. (conclusion)[1]

Moreover, the *African* in African-American linguistic experiences, as researchers have attested, cannot be rightfully denied (Turner 1949; Dalby 1972; Holloway and Vass 1993). We most likely want to retain all of our *bads* that mean *good*, constructions derived from West African languages, as linguist Geneva Smitherman informs us (1977, pp. 59–60). In Mandingo, the phrase *a ka nyi ko-jugu* literally means "it is good badly" or, in other words, "it is very good"

(Smitherman, 1977, p. 44). The attraction, then, to the Greek classical art is most productively expressed as an embrace of its ethical dimensions.

The tale of origins is familiar. Rhetoric in the Western world formed as a discipline in the aftermath of dissolved monarchies in the fifth century BCE. Citizens of a fledgling democracy had to learn to make legal claims on redistributed lands and to conduct civic business overall. Informal training and formal academies fostered development of the required skills, which led to eloquent and compelling displays of reasoning in public forums. It also led to the oft-cited criticism of rhetoric by Plato contained in *Gorgias*, in which the virtues of the truth-seeking philosopher are posed against the wily rhetorician who shamefully only "aims at what is pleasant, ignoring the good" (247). In any event, Greek rhetoric mainly flourished as an art and, subsequently, as a body of rules, and it morphed into, among other varieties, Roman, British, and American traditions.

Because the African-American saga intersected with the historical movement sketched above primarily through the institution of enslavement, the rhetoric of African Americans, before they were even named such, evinced broader imperatives than Platonic thought. Some Black people certainly needed to speak well in public and legal forums, but most desired to do more, namely, obtain the legal status of being free. They felt no need to theorize away the potency of verbal skills that could aid a politically liberating process. When one considers *Gorgias* alongside the attack in *Phaedrus* on literacy (pp. 519–21) and the denigrating of poetry in *Republic* (pp. 821–33), one realizes that some of the strongest currents in Plato's work theoretically surge against rhetoricians and against a historical Black agenda, for education, literacy, freedom, and poetry are unbreakably linked for African Americans.

For example, many African Americans valued the nineteenth-century poet James Whitfield (1853/1998). Writing during the antebellum period, Whitfield expresses, in "America," the desire to abolish slavery:

> But in the sacred name of peace,
> > Of justice, virtue, love and truth,
> We pray, and never mean to cease,
> > Till weak old age and fiery youth
> In freedom's cause their voices raise,
> And burst the bonds of every slave;
> Till, north and south, and east and west,
> The wrongs we bear shall be redressed.
> > (p. 381)

Thus, Whitfield makes an argument through verse for a better conception and practice of nationhood. Rather than adhering to any injunction against poetry, he protests through poetry in the name of truth and *as* the truth. His work is reflective of *Nommo*, the traditional African belief in the visionary, creative, and community-building capacity of the performed word (Asante and Robb, 1971, p. 2; Asante, 1972, pp. 371–2; Smitherman, 1977, p. 78).

The existential gestures in the folk lyrics of "Wild Negro Bill" make a similar point, though in a less genteel and more badman or gangsta-like manner:

> I'se wild Nigger Bill
> Frum Redpepper Hill.
> I never did wo'k, an' I never will.
>
> I'se done killed de Boss.
> I'se knocked down de hoss.
> I eats up raw goose widout apple sauce!
>
> I'se Run-a-way Bill,
> I knows dey mought kill;
> But ole Mosser hain't cotch me, an' he never will!
>
> (p. 7)

Furthermore, the academically expressed suspicions or devaluations of rhetoric, mainly deconstructionist fare about the arbitrariness of the sign, the instability of language, the impossibility of language representing agency and conveying immutably specified meaning, and the superiority of science could never gain more than a tentative foothold in Black strivings.[2] The play of language, its vibrant quality, has always been essential to African Americans, and we have never been overly disturbed by the ideas that language constructs us and is subjective. We have known that language is not the *only* thing that constructs us, and we have taken language subjectivity as a given to be engaged by means of the agency that we know that we possess.

In "John in Jail," a tale in the well-known John-and-Old-Master genre, we encounter the following scenario:

> One time Old Boss get a call from the sheriff, say that John was in jail and did Old Boss want him out on bail. Old Boss, he was mad that John give him so much trouble, but he got to get John out cause they was work to be done. So he went down to the sheriff's place and put ten dollars on the line, sign some papers and take John home with him.
>
> "How come they put you in jail?" the Boss say.
>
> "'Spect it was 'count of Miss Elizabeth's petunias," John say.
>
> "Old Elizabeth Grant? What's her petunias got to do with it?" Old Boss say.
>
> "I hear tell Miss Elizabeth want a man to trim up her petunia garden," John say. "I got a little time now and then between workin' in the field, so I went up there to Miss Elizabeth's place to see could she use me. I knock on the back door and Miss Elizabeth come and ask me what I want. I tell her

I'm the man to work in her petunia garden. She ask to see my testimonials, and that's when I make my mistake."

(p. 440)

But perhaps John has not erred. As he flirts with a racial and sexual taboo, the ambiguity of language and his manipulation of it, along with his status as a valued worker, afford him safety despite his misstep in asserting manhood. Strangely enough, *testimonial* and *testicle* both stem from the Latin word *testis*. Perhaps John understands the system after all. He would be credible claiming confusion and a lack of linguistic command. He benefits from the slipperiness of interpretation.

Novelist Walter Mosley (2008) also illustrates that African Americans are not unduly disturbed about the instability of language. In *The Right Mistake*, the third installment of his Socrates Fortlow series, Socrates hosts a weekly Thinkers' Meeting at his home, a venue dubbed The Big Nickel. At one of the evening gatherings, Socrates initiates a discussion about identity politics that lasts beyond 5:00 AM the next morning. During the heated exchange, punctuated with the different views of group members about what defines Blackness, Socrates argues that Blackness is merely a social construction: "There's ain't no black men and women, no African-Americans in this room, there's just people with names and ages and features" (220). But in the morning, when one of the participants, Mustafa Ali, asks Socrates why, given Socrates's position, he still uses the labels *black people* and *white people*. "Because," Socrates replies, "them words is still usin' me, Brother Ali. They usin' me like a mothafuckah" (222). The streetwise Socrates acknowledges both the complexity and material power of language, as well as some of the contradictions that arise.

At a more formal level, Frederick Douglass, as have legions of lawyers and judges, understood that the very Constitution could be interpreted in various ways. When he was an uncompromising abolitionist in the mold of William Lloyd Garrison, Douglass considered the Constitution to be strictly a pro-slavery document given several provisions: 1) the phrase "three fifths of all other Persons" (Article 1, Section 2), by which 60 percent of the enslaved population was counted relative to the apportioning of seats in the House of Representatives; 2) "calling forth the Militia to execute the Laws of the Union, suppress insurrections and repel invasions" (Article 1, Section 8), said by many to refer directly to slave uprisings; 3) "the Migration or Importation of such Persons as any of the States now existing shall think proper to admit, shall not be prohibited by the Congress prior to the Year one thousand eight hundred and eight" (Article 1, Section 9), which effectively extended the slave trade twenty years; and 4) "no Person held to Service or Labour in one State, under the Laws thereof, escaping into another, shall, in Consequence of any Law or Regulation therein, be discharged from such Service or Labour, but shall be delivered up on Claim of the Party to whom such Service or Labour may be due" (Article 4, Section 2), which mandated the return of fugitive slaves on the demand of slaveholders.

At a convention in 1850, Douglass asserted, "I hold that to swear to support a constitution which requires us to put down slave insurrections and send back fugitive slaves is a sin. It is a sin to swear to support that which is sin—which can require us to sin ("Is the Constitution Pro-Slavery?" p. 221). He declared further, "To say that the constitution is Anti-Slavery is an assumption against an overwhelming array of testimony and against the Constitution itself" (p. 231). To Douglass, it was "*irresistibly clear*" that the Constitution, partly written by slave-holders, promoted slavery in spirit and substance. He evoked the religious doctrine of transubstantiation to argue that although the word *slave* was not mentioned in the Constitution, the legitimation of slavery existed there in reality (p. 232).[3]

As time went on, Douglass became keenly interested in and supportive of the anti-slavery advocacy unfolding inside the Free Soil and Republican parties. He then regarded the Constitution as an anti-slavery instrument because he believed that linking it to the moral high ground and then siding with it made his own anti-slavery argument more acceptable to the public that he addressed (Howard-Pitney, 1990, p. 41). Eschewing the Garrisonian line, Douglass no longer saw advantage in railing against the Constitution. In his 1860 speech in Glasgow titled "The American Constitution and the Slave," he put positive spins on the alleged pro-slavery clauses. For example, the three-fifths compromise became reasonable to him because it meant fewer congressional representatives for slaveholding states than if the enslaved were counted as full persons. He averred,

> instead of encouraging slavery, the constitution encourages freedom, by *holding out to every slaveholding State the inducement of an increase of two-fifths of political power by becoming a free State.* So much for the three-fifths clause; taking it at its worst, it still leans to freedom, not to slavery.
>
> (p. 352, emphasis original)

Concerning the so-called provision for quelling slave insurrections, Douglass argued that the language of Section 8 of Article 1 is not specific to slave rebellions but speaks to riots or insurrections in general. Thus, in his view, no such thing as a slave-insurrection clause actually exists in the Constitution (pp. 354–5). Similarly, Douglass contended that the framers of the Constitution were following the conventional wisdom that the slave trade was the lifeblood of the institution of slavery and, therefore, intended for slavery to end rather than to be perpetuated after the abolishment of the slave trade. The Founding Fathers, the logic unfolded, planned for the more perfect union to be slave free; indeed, ratifying the abolition clause was the price of admission (pp. 353–4). Moreover, Douglass pointed out, nothing in the Constitution forbade the abolishing of slavery altogether (p. 365).

Discussing the putative fugitive-slave clause, Douglass believed that it only applied to indentured servants and apprentices. Enslaved workers were not legally able to enter into contracts; therefore, they could not owe any labor contractually. He concluded that slaves were legally exempt from the clause (pp. 355–9).

Once Douglass had settled on his revised positions, which he had done prior to his appearance in Glasgow, he ironically insisted on literal readings of the Constitution. He declared, "It is no vague, indefinite, floating, unsubstantial something, called, according to any man's fancy, now a weasel, now a whale. But it is something substantial. It is a plainly written document; not in Hebrew nor Greek, but in English" (pp. 346–7). He no longer talked about transubstantiation or of properly engaging the text to render meaning beyond restricted representations, and he made a distinction between a bad government and a good governing document (pp. 345, 349).

We will not adjudicate the matter of earlier Douglass versus later Douglass. Obviously, intelligent arguments can still be made on both sides of the issue. Our point is to emphasize, through presenting a set of transactions by an extremely astute practitioner of rhetoric and literacy, the African-American investment in strategic language and to suggest that Africans Americans generally understand rhetorical and/or literate practices to be competitive arenas and have been more disposed to participate in them enthusiastically than to ruminate philosophically about the inadequacy of verbal forms. They start with the understanding that, for example, *perfect day* connotes something different for everyone. Or as Douglass (1857/1985) said when challenged to a debate by the fabulously talented Black orator Charles Lenox Remond, "It will give me infinite pleasure to meet Mr. Remond in debate on the question. Coffee and pistols for two!" (p. 150).

Beyond relishing and mastering various modes of folkloric expression and debate, Blacks made three distinctive and stupendous rhetorical contributions by the end of the nineteenth century. They had generated hundreds of slave narratives, tales that undergird the entire tradition of African-American literature. They had verbally constituted the group of people known as African Americans, a crucial development in political progress. In addition, they had created a musical tradition rooted in spirituals and blues that formed a stirring articulation of Black yearnings and has served as an eloquent and enduring argument for Black humanity.

Narrating Black Freedom

Approximately 100 life stories written or dictated by fugitive or former slaves were published between 1760 and the end of the Civil War in 1865. They powerfully linked the ideas of being, literacy, and freedom. Over time, as Bernard Bell (1987) pointed out, speeches on the lecture platform at anti-slavery meetings become remodeled as written renditions such as Frederick Douglass' popular and influential *Narrative of the Life of Frederick Douglass, An American Slave, Written by Himself* (1845). Bell explained:

> Most knew that antislavery meetings would generally begin with introductory remarks by a local abolitionist in preparation for the appearance of a seasoned guest lecturer like Garrison or a fugitive like Douglass to provide

a dramatic account of life in bondage. This performance would be followed by an impassioned, critical analysis of the evils of the Peculiar Institution and, on occasion, either a few songs or poems. Finally, a collection for the cause would be taken up, abolition publications sold, and the meeting adjourned.

(Bell, p. 28)

James Olney (1985) provided a related six-part outline:

1. a portrait signed by the narrator;
2. a title page featuring the actual phrase or some variant of "written by himself;"
3. testimonials, prefaces, or introductions by white abolitionists, amanuenses, or editors verifying that the tale is truthful though perhaps an understatement regarding the horrors of enslavement;
4. a poetic epigraph;
5. the narrative proper, which includes stock features such as an opening assertion "I was born," a brief and sometimes vague account of parentage, details of authoritarian cruelty, descriptions of both failed and successful escape attempts, the taking of a new surname, and reflections on the system of enslavement;
6. appended documentary material such as bills of sale and newspaper clippings, further reflections, appeals to readers for moral and financial support for anti-slavery initiatives, as well as the inclusion of poems, speeches, and sermons.

(pp. 152–3)

In addition, a salient feature of antebellum slave narratives is the trope of the talking book/silent book, a development treated most fully by Henry Louis Gates, Jr. (1998). Books announce, authorize, and mark communities, speaking to masters and remaining mum toward the enslaved. The prototypical example occurs in Gronniosaw's *A Narrative of the Most Remarkable Particulars in the Life of James Albert Ukasaw Gronniosaw, an African Prince, as Related by Himself* (1770/1998):

[My master] used to read prayers in public to the ship's crew every Sabbath day; and when I first saw him read, I was never so surprised in my whole life as when I saw the book talk to my master; for I thought it did, as I observed him to look upon it, and move his lips—I wished it would do so to me.—As soon as my master had done reading I followed him to the place where he put the book, being mightily delighted with it, and when nobody saw me, I opened it and put my ear down close upon it, in great hope that it would say something to me; but I was very sorry and greatly disappointed when I found it would not speak; this thought immediately presented itself to me, that everybody and everything despised me because I was black.

(pp. 40–1)

Ironically, for Gronniosaw, the prayer book acted as Plato said it would. It was unable to represent itself. To the philosopher, the slave should not have been disappointed because there was no true knowledge to be gained from a non-dialogic string of words. Even if Plato granted the possibility that true knowledge could exist in such a book—a likely concession on his part that would indicate, as language scholar James Paul Gee notes in "Legacies of Literacy" (1988, pp. 199–201), the basic contradiction in Plato's thinking—he would not necessarily have trusted Gronniosaw, a slave presumably fitted by nature to be one, to grasp it. But Gronniosaw has no patience for such ideas, and books become central to his journey.

Olaudah Equiano, an acquaintance of Gronniosaw's, extended the trope of the talking book/silent book in the first slave narrative to receive wide international acclaim. In the *Interesting Narrative of the Life of Olaudah Equiano, or Gustavus Vassa, the African, Written by Himself* (1789), he relates:

> I had often seen my master and Dick employed in reading; and I had great curiosity to talk to the books, as I thought they did; and so to learn how all things had a beginning: for that purpose I have often taken up a book, and have talked to it, and then put my ears to it, when alone, in hopes it would answer me; and I had been very much concerned when I found it remained silent.
>
> (p. 68)

Like Gronniosaw, Equiano transformed through literacy the dynamic of silence into a heralded quest for liberation. He does more than help to develop a textual trope and convey yearnings of individual freedom; he provides a text that self-consciously reflects the desire for social freedom. Although the free Equiano in his forties was not very African culturally (as an adult he never used the name Oaudah Equiano except in his book), he realized that much of the hardship he had suffered had to do with responses to his physical Africaness. Thus, as the leading Black abolitionist in England, he framed his book as an anti-slavery petition to the House of Parliament. His social consciousness was revealed in his first-person-plural descriptions of Africans:

1. We are almost a nation of dancers, musicians, and poets.

    (p. 34)

2. As our manners are simple, our luxuries are few.

    (p. 34)

3. Our manner of living is entirely plain.

    (p. 35)

4. In our buildings we study convenience rather than ornament.

    (p. 36)

The notable exception is when Equiano mentions religion. The convert to Christianity refers to what *natives* believe in—"a Creator who lives in the sun, and is girted round with a belt that he may never eat or drink; but, according to some, he smokes a pipe" (p. 40). Equiano takes himself out of that particular picture, but overall he has positioned himself rhetorically, in accord with the book's title, as African.

At the close of the narrative Equiano makes a direct appeal in letter form to Queen Charlotte of England: "Yet I do not solicit your royal pity for my own distress: my sufferings, although numerous, are in a measure forgotten. I supplicate your Majesty's compassion for millions of my African countrymen, who groan under the lash of tyranny in the West Indies" (p. 231). He signs his letter, "Gustavus Vassa, The Oppressed Ethiopian" (232). Despite being on his way to becoming a wealthy Briton, he intends his autobiography to undermine the slave trade and slavery itself. His *I* is ultimately a *we*.

Perhaps a direct offspring of *The Interesting Narrative*, Harriet Jacobs's *Incidents in the Life of a Slave Girl* (1861/1973) shares the strong sense of *we-ness* and the call for liberation. Her concern for community was so strong that she used a pseudonym (Linda Brent) and concealed names and places to protect others. Not wanting to seem self-important, she makes the same overture to humility that Equiano does. She describes herself as inadequate to the task and so forth, but she is also bold in her political pronouncements:

> I have not written my experiences in order to attract attention to myself; on the contrary, it would have been more pleasant to me to have been silent about my own history. Neither do I care to excite sympathy for my own sufferings. But I do earnestly desire to arouse the women of the North to a realizing sense of the condition of two millions of women at the South, still in bondage, suffering from what I suffered, and most of them far worse. I want to add my testimony to that of abler pens to convince the people of the Free States what Slavery really is. Only by experience can any one realize how deep, and dark, and foul is the pit of abominations. May the blessing of God rest on this imperfect on behalf of my persecuted people!
>
> (p. xiv)

Jacobs constructs a self that proffers a compelling vision of activism. And not leaving the narrative line open for just any interpretation, she habitually disrupts it to deliver lectures. For example, considering the constriction of Black girlhood in the slavocracy vis-à-vis the opportunities afforded to White girlhood, Jacobs asks, "In view of these things, why are ye silent, ye free men and women of the north? Why do your tongues falter in maintenance of the right?" (p. 29).

Further expounding on morality, particularly the inadequate actions of religious institutions, she exhorts:

> They send the Bible to heathen abroad, and neglect the heathen at home. I am glad that missionaries go out to the dark corners of the earth; but I

ask them not to overlook the dark corners at home. Talk to American slaveholders as you talk to savages in Africa. Tell *them* it is wrong to traffic in men. Tell them it is sinful to sell their own children, and atrocious to violate their own daughters. Tell them that all men are brethren, and that man has no right to shut out the light of knowledge from his brother. Tell them they are answerable to God for sealing up the Fountain of Life from souls that are thirsting for it.

(pp. 75–6).

Along with her lectures, Jacobs remarks about some of the crafty Black rhetors that she encounters. One such person is Luke, whom she had known in South Carolina. When she runs into him up North, she wonders how he has obtained the funds to enact his plan of traveling to Canada. Luke assures her that he had the matter in hand:

I'd bin workin all my days fur dem cussed whites, an got no pay but kicks and cuffs. So I tought dis nigger had a right to money nuff to bring him to de Free States. Massa Henry he lib till ebery body vish him dead; and ven he did die, I knowed de debbil would hab him, an vouldn't vant him to bring his money 'long too. So I tuk some of his bills, and put 'em in de pocket of his ole trousers. An ven he was buried, dis nigger ask fur dem ole trousers, an dey gub 'em to me. . . . You see I didn't *steal* it; dey *gub* it to me.

(p. 198)

Luke was a forerunner in understanding the acute need for epistemic breaks, and he constructed a rhetorical world that balanced his moral sense, just as his moral sense also shaped his rhetorical outlook. As she editorializes, Jacobs endorses Luke's perspective:

When a man has his wages stolen from him, year after year, and the laws sanction and enforce the theft, how can he be expected to have more regard for honesty that has the man that robs him? I have become somewhat enlightened, but I confess that I agree with poor, ignorant, muchabused Luke, in thinking he had a *right* to that money, as a portion of his unpaid wages.

(p. 198)

Jacobs astutely assesses individual behavior in the context of the broader political and socioeconomic network of slavery. As a narrator, she continues to wield the social *I*.

Neo-slave narratives written decades, even more than a century, later evince a similar commitment to the social *I*. *The Autobiography of Malcolm X* (1965a) is a case in point. Malcolm sought to relate a story of his life, among several possible versions, that best showed his opposition to White supremacy and his allegiance to African Americans. He and his collaborator Alex Haley were keenly aware of the social and selective nature of their work. After all, Malcolm had written in his notebook as a twelve-year-old schoolboy that he wanted to be a rhetorician, a less-told tale than the one about his being discouraged from being an attorney and encouraged to become a carpenter.[4]

One of the points of contention that arose between the two men occurred when Malcolm, after his highly-publicized separation from the Nation of Islam, wanted to revise early sections of the manuscript to diminish the impact in the story of Elijah Muhammad, giving him less credit for his, Malcolm's, spiritual and intellectual growth. Haley, in his epilogue, recounts their debate. He tried to change Malcolm's mind because Haley did not want the book to be a polemic against Elijah Muhammad. A gruff Malcolm asked at one juncture, "Whose book is this?" (p. 421). Haley prevailed, for the better we believe. But the point we want to emphasize is that Malcolm X did not ask, "Whose life is this?" No, he knew that the story—*whose book?*—had the potential for greater impact and was also a complicated matter unto itself. As he relates in "1965," the final chapter of the book, "I have given to this book so much of whatever time I have because I feel, and I hope, that if I honestly and fully tell my life's account, read objectively it might prove to be a testimony of some social value" (p. 386). That sentence is the book's great understatement, for it is hard to imagine that Malcolm's legacy would be as great as it is without *The Autobiography* and such statements as the following:

> I believe that it would be almost impossible to find anywhere in America a black man who has lived further down in the mud of human society than I have; or a black man who has been any more ignorant than I have been; or a black man who has suffered more anguish during his life than I have. But it is only after the deepest darkness that the greatest joy can come; it is only after slavery and prison that the sweetest appreciation of freedom can come.
>
> For the freedom of my 22 million black brothers and sisters here in America, I do believe that I have fought the best that I knew how, and the best that I know how, and the best that I could, with the shortcomings that I have. I know that my shortcomings are many.
>
> (p. 387)

One could even argue feasibly, given Malcolm's relative disregard for the danger he was in, that he began to shape his life to fit the story, to prepare for his death by preparing the most enduring tale of his life, replete with echoes of Olaudah Equiano and Harriet Jacobs.

Naming in the Dark

In addition to the publishing and reading of narratives, other everyday acts of rhetorical identification have been crucial to Black liberation efforts. Any Black person looking to claim a home in the United States has likely understood at one time or another Malcolm X's startling use of the trope of chiasmus: "We didn't land on Plymouth Rock; the rock was landed on us" (1964).[5] Black location and identity have always been precarious. Rhetoric scholar Dexter B. Gordon (2003), without the specter of falling debris, addressed the question of identity formation:

> A ready example is the identity of "African American," which is constructed as the re-articulation of the "African," one belonging to the continent of Africa, and the "American," one belonging to the United States. This became necessary because the subject position of "African," while it affirmed a black heritage, made it difficult for blacks to claim a place in the United States. On the other hand, while "American" pointed to a subject belonging to the United States, its strong Anglo connotations implied a negation of the black heritage.
>
> (p. 35)

Similarly, Toni Morrison (1992) articulates, "Deep within the word "American" is its association with race. . . . American means white, and Africanist people struggle to make the term applicable to themselves with ethnicity and hyphen after hyphen after hyphen (p. 47).

But the association has been on the surface as well. White supremacist rhetoric such as Robert Walsh's pro-slavery tract *An Appeal from the Judgements of Great Britain Respecting the United States of America* (1819) circulated widely and was intended to normalize discursively the system of black enslavement. The rationale of such rhetoric consisted of what Gordon termed the "five tenets of oppression," namely:

1. constitution of a servile collective Black subject.
2. collective Black subject as white property.
3. slavery as an institution that developed the important value of liberty and property among citizens [with Blacks as property and as noncitizens].
4. slavery as a mechanism to foster [from a white supremacist perspective] the reform of Blacks.
5. slavery as a perpetual institution and Blacks as natural slaves.

(pp. 67–8).

Within this discursive territory, Black abolitionists forged a constitutive and countering rhetoric to spur Black collective action.

Blacks were not unfamiliar operating politically in concert with one another. After all, Gabriel Prosser reportedly organized almost a thousand slaves for a rebellion in 1800.[6] But they lacked in Gordon's view a broad sense of peoplehood. He understood that New World Africans possessed no significant sense of themselves as a homogenous group whether prior to or in the years of the early Republic. They shared a commonality of social conditions, widespread enslavement obviously being the most salient, but the facts of servitude and suffering did not constitute a consciously realized political identity or result yet in the "birth of the black public subject" (p. 70). Thus, abolitionist rhetors began to appeal to the "essential" realities of Blackness: African ancestry and American enslavement. As a practice of rhetorical materialism, they used language to shape identity. Prototypical texts include Robert Alexander Young's *The Ethiopian Manifesto* (1829/2001). Establishing that his work required the attention of "those proceeding in descent from the Ethiopian or African people," he contended that way for them to secure the rights bestowed by God "exacts the convocation of ourselves in a body politic" 85–86). On the heels of Young, David Walker (1829/1965) pitched his *Appeal* to an audience he hoped would function as a unified group, namely, "the coloured citizens of the world," particularly those in the United States. Walker reminded his readers that the God of the Ethiopians is pleased by cries against racial oppression but that for deliverance the oppressed must be disposed to embrace freedom.

The references to Ethiopia, a term used synonymous with "Africa" by Young and Walker as well as by Equiano, who represented himself to Queen Charlotte as "the Oppressed Ethiopian," are expressions of an important trope of identity in African-American and Afro-Atlantic rhetoric. Spurred by biblical prophecy, most notably Psalms 68:31 with its declaration that "Princes shall come out of Egypt; Ethiopia shall soon stretch out her hands unto God," many in the African diaspora have viewed the idea of Ethiopia as a symbol of past African glory and as a prediction of Black resurgence or even conquest. In addition, many African Americans took pride in the fact that Ethiopia was the only African nation to repel a European military and remain sovereign while Europeans colonized most of the remaining continent. For some, in the 1930s, the invasion of Ethiopia by Italy was the most important international cause. The imperative to defeat Italian imperialism was linked intellectually and viscerally to the battle against anti-Black racism in the United States (Putnam, 2012).

Distinct from the religious movements or churches in Africa, particularly in South Africa, Ethiopianism in the West, according to Moses (1975),

> may be defined as the effort of the English-speaking Black or African person to view his past enslavement and present cultural dependency in terms of the broader history of civilization. It serves to remind him that this present scientific technological civilization, dominated by Western Europe for a scant four hundred years, will go under certainly—like all the empires of the past.

(p. 416)

For Moses, then, Ethiopianism in African-American culture combines the Rising Africa Theme with a story about the Decline of the West (p. 414). We see both components evident in the work of Walker, who forecasts uplift by the God of the Ethiopians and also prophesizes the doom of the oppressors (p. 3).

Maria Stewart (1833/2001), the first African-American women to address a mixed audience of men and women in public, invoked the Rising Africa Theme as she spoke of the plight of her people:

> History informs us that we sprung from one of the most learned nations of the whole earth; from the seat, if not the parent of science; yes, poor, despised Africa was once the resort of sages and legislators of other nations, was esteemed the school for learning, and the most illustrious men in Greece flocked thither for instruction, But it was our gross sink and abominations that provoked the Almighty to frown thus heavily upon us, and give our glory unto others. Sin and prodigality have caused the downfall of nations, kings and emperors; and were it not that God in wrath remembers mercy, we might indeed despair; but a promise is left us; "Ethiopia shall again stretch forth her hands unto God."
>
> (p. 124)

Stewart was less aggressive than Walker in charging European aggression with the moral crime of slavery, but she was nonetheless a fervent abolitionist and saw abolitionist activity as essential to redeeming the promise.

Prominent poets like Frances E. W. Harper (1854/1988), Paul Laurence Dunbar (1896/1993), and Langston Hughes (1920/1994) affirmed in verse the sentiments of Young, Walker, Stewart, and many others. In "Ethiopia," Harper writes:

> Yes! Ethiopia yet shall stretch
>   Her bleeding hands abroad;
> Her cry of agony shall reach
>   The burning throne of God.
>
> The tyrant's yoke from off her neck,
>   His fetters from her soul
> The mighty hand of God shall break,
>   And spurn the base control.
> ("Ethiopia," pp. 7–8)

Near the turn of the century, fellow poet Dunbar followed suit with "Ode to Ethiopia," and a generation later, Langston Hughes, though not using the term Ethiopia, paid tribute to Africa in "The Negro Speaks of Rivers."

In the twentieth century, Marcus Garvey was the person who most famously embodied the Rising Africa Theme. His embrace of not simply the legacy of the Ethiopian empire and the overarching African past but of the modern nation-state and its head, Haile Selassie, was crucial to the development of Rastafarianism, perhaps the most popular practice of Ethiopianism in the contemporary Afro-Atlantic world. In its strongest version, Rastafarianism posits Salassie, who visited Jamaica in 1966, as divine and Ethiopia as *the* homeland to which a return is the most desirable goal. In a weaker version, the envisioned return is mental and cultural; pan-African solidarity is more the point. In either case, the ethos has been expressed by latter-day analogs to Harper and Dunbar, most famously Jamaican songwriter and singer Bob Marley with entries like "Africa Unite," which addresses glorious unification, or the Rising Africa Theme, and an exit from The Declining West, or as Marley phrases it, Babylon.

Spiritual and Blue

The more than 6,000 Negro Spirituals, as they are generally called, also powerfully express pain, hope, and faith. They brilliantly blend experiences in the American slavocracy, particularly the exposure to Protestant Christianity and the King James Bible, with structural patterns, sonic textures, and themes of African creative discourse. The remarkable achievement has inspired generations of African-American artists. Numerous songs, poems, plays, and fictional works rely on the spirituals and the related biblical stories for content, plot, and style.

No one assessment of the spirituals predominates; scholars and laypersons still debate vigorously the exact nature of their structure and import.[7] The precise advent of the spirituals is a matter of dispute as well.[8] But it can reasonably be argued that captured Africans were analyzing and commenting on their social plight, as well as melding expressive forms, from the beginnings of the Middle Passage. Certain is that they did not leave their African culture entirely behind. African epics and praise poems inform spirituals like "Go Down, Moses" (an epic) and "Joshua Fit de Battle of Jericho" (a praise poem). As the editors of *The Riverside Anthology of the African American Literary Tradition* explained, "the spirituals reflect the African heroic epic in form, content, and performance style. The African oral epic consists of long narrative recitations and songs interwoven with praise poems, chants, sermons, hymns, prayers and improvisations" (p. 35). "Go Down, Moses," the most popular spiritual and the first to be written down according to scholar Richard Newman (1998, p. 68), bears a strong structural resemblance to *Sunjata* (also spelled *Sundiata*), an epic poem from the Mandingo tradition. *Sunjata*, which dates back to the thirteenth century, describes the exploits of the hero who orchestrated the rise of the Mali Empire. Sunjata overcomes obstacles, neutralizes his archenemy, and ascends to prominence. As is typical in African epics, his triumph is made possible through sorcery, not simply brute strength. This is similar to Moses, who, favored by his God, can command plagues and part the waters. Thus, while stilled steeped in African culture and notwithstanding the fact that the Bible represented the religion of the enslavers, Africans were attracted to biblical heroes as well as to visions of an ultimately just God and of divine deliverance. The spirituals established the metaphor of the antebellum South as the American Egypt—with Blacks the chosen and enslaved people laboring under an evil Pharoah and, most important, capable of producing a Moses.

Although not all spirituals overtly encode politics like "Go Down, Moses," a notable number express politics nonetheless. The songs contain numerous coded messages about rebellion and escape. "Swing Low, Sweet Chariot" may have signaled the arrival of the Underground Railroad. "Steal Away to Jesus" may have similarly announced an escape attempt. It has been surmised that "God's Going to Trouble the Water" was employed by Harriet Tubman to caution runaways to travel by water as much as possible in order to confuse bloodhounds. Undeniably, all kinds of movement are conveyed in the songs—by way of chariots, trains, the Gospel ship, even foot—to suggest meaning beyond the concern of a soul's passage to heaven.

The blues, a secular, raw, and sometimes profane counterpart to the spirituals, embrace the vicissitudes of life with special attention to the hard times. Not a music of resignation or ultimate despair, as some may imagine, the blues are better thought of as poignant and sobering recognition that there will always be more obstacles to overcome. Commenting on the blues, James Cone (1992) asserted, "they are not propositional truths *about* the Black experience. Rather they are the essential ingredients that define the *essence* of the Black experience. And to understand them, it is necessary to view the blues as *a state of mind in relation to the Truth of the Black experience*" (p. 102). Or as the narrator of James Baldwin's well-known short story "Sonny's Blues" (1957/1995) realizes when watching his piano-playing brother, who has battled drug addiction and from whom he has been estranged, perform in a club,

> while the tale of how we suffer, and how we are delighted, and how we may triumph is never new, it always must be heard. There isn't any other tale to tell, it's the only light we've got in all this darkness.
>
> (p. 139)

It is generally acknowledged that the blues originated on Southern plantations and derived from the spirituals, chants, work songs, and dance music. Whatever the specifics of the origin narrative, there no is debating the wide influence of the blues and its offshoots. For our purposes, the most relevant consideration is the rhetorical work that these forms of music do.

"What You Know About That, Melvin?"

Near the close of the film *Baby Boy* (2001), as the character Jody Summers leaves his mother's residence, he passes her boyfriend Melvin, who is in the driveway talking with a friend who helps him (Melvin) with his landscaping business. Jody and Melvin chat briefly:

> "How you doing, Baby Boy?"
> "Enjoying this California lifestyle. Take care of my mama."
> "I'm on the case."

This conversation is far more than a casual exchange of pleasantries. It signifies Jody's emergence into manhood, which puts him on par with other men. While a twenty-year-old mama's boy still living at home, he resisted the presence of Melvin, who moved into the home and undercut the relationship in which Jody was overly dependent on his mother Juanita and considered it her primary duty to attend to many of his wants. Meanwhile, Jody has felt free to father children—two sons—without making serious commitments to either of their mothers. One of them, Yvette, is his girlfriend, though he is not faithful to her. Jody does possess redeeming qualities; we see him hustling women's clothes to make money, spending time with his children, worrying about his mother's safety, and, after being tempted, rejecting a sexual invitation from one of Yvette's co-workers. And he is ultimately salvageable because he has not embraced the violence of thug life. But the balance of his disposition ledger clearly indicates immaturity and irresponsibility.

Jody frames his refusal to move out as fear that he will be killed like his elder brother, who met such fate after being forced from the home. No correlation seems to exist, however, between living in one's childhood home and avoiding death. In fact, Jody escapes an assassination attempt, and it would be far-fetched to attribute his survival to the fact that he still lived with his mother. Melvin favors a competing explanation, thinking in pop-psychological terms that Jody suffers from an Oedipus complex that he needs to outgrow. He purposely constricts Jody's comfort zone as much as he can. Although a flawed person himself, an ex-gangbanging felon with a history of domestic abuse, he is clearly repentant, kind to Juanita, and certainly no boy.

The tension between Jody and Melvin escalates into a one-punch TKO with Jody predictably on the losing end, but the two bond when Melvin subsequently helps Jody to deal with the aftermath of an explosive episode in the streets that resulted in the death of Rodney, a rival who had tormented Yvette, taken over her apartment, which could only have happened in Jody's absence, and made the aforementioned attempt on Jody's life. It is the acceptance of Melvin's counsel—manly counsel—that makes Jody a member of the club that Melvin would have him join. As a result, the two can converse as equals in the front yard. Jody is now only ironically Baby Boy, and his voice can be the voice of wisdom and instruction to other men.

After Jody starts the car, we hear GQ's "I Do Love You" (1979). He asks, "What you know about that, Melvin? This is grown folks music."

"That's what I'm talking about," responds Melvin while bobbing his head.

Jody is not really questioning his elder. When Melvin first heard the original version of the song, the classic Billy Stewart rendition (1965), he would have been about Jody's present age, and Jody would not even have been born. Jody is rhetorically affirming his newfound maturity through old-school rhythm and blues, music even more resonantly old-school than perhaps he realizes. He has evolved beyond being indifferent or hostile to his mother's advice—because it suggested mature love and happiness for her—to appreciate a crooning Marvin Gaye as typified by "Just to Keep You Satisfied" (1973). He has gone from sitting in his bedroom with a giant likeness of Tupac Shakur, definitely no rhythm-and-blues crooner, whatever admirable things he was, to embracing expressions of unfailing love and devotion that symbolize the best of a past, present, and future Black world. "I Do Love You" plays in the background and months transpire in filmic time as Jody displays his keys to the apartment he now shares with Yvette and their son JoJo, snuggles up to Yvette, eventually (off screen) marries her, fathers a third child (a reversal of the abortion scene near the beginning of the movie), and protectively takes Yvette and JoJo on an outing to a local park. With director John Singleton assuming the music controls, Jody continues to earn the song's stamp of approval, to live up to, in other words, the song's lyrics. Music historian Jonathan Friedman (2015) writes, "Lyrics give musical sounds a specific character, turning a notoriously abstract medium into a delivery system for potential crystal clarity . . . songs are uniquely adept at compressing, containing and conveying streamlined concepts" (pp. 73–4). Jody's manhood is calibrated not simply through acts of fatherhood and marriage but through the metered stanzas, recurring phrases, clichés, choruses, and rhyme of rhythm-and-blues rhetoric (74). Both character and director negotiate a Black urban landscape and transfigure elements of that environment into moments of Black love and Black triumph and into explanations of those triumphs, attestations about that love, and suggestions for growth. This is all standard work in the African-American rhetorical tradition.

Notes

1. In *Prior Analytics*, Aristotle discusses the syllogism as a form of deductive reasoning (pp. 4–9). There are several forms of the syllogism, but it is often represented as three related propositions in a major premise-minor premise-conclusion format. If the major and minor premises are both true and properly aligned, the conclusion is valid, as in our example. The enthymeme, which is discussed by Aristotle in *On Rhetoric* (pp. 33–4), is essentially a syllogism in which premises might be unstated. The actual enthymeme in the Tavares song is "Heaven must be missin' an angel/ Missin' one angel, child/'Cause you're here with me right now." That all angels live in heaven and that "you" are one are propositions that, as indicated, are implied.
2. Jennifer Richards (2008, pp. 114–56) examines these issues in a far-ranging discussion that includes reviewing key positions by I. A. Richards (1936); Ferdinand de Saussure (1916/1966); Gérard Genette (1982); Roland Barthes (1988); Jacques Derrida (2004); and Paul de Man (1979, 1982, 1986).
3. Transubstantiation, a controversial idea even in Christian circles, is the belief that consecrated bread and wine are not merely symbolic of Christ's body and blood but are in fact the real presence of that body and blood. The passage from the Bible most often linked with transubstantiation and its justification is John 6:32–58.
4. On a page titled "Career Chart," Malcolm did write a list of what he called basic terminal jobs. Those were lawyer, district attorney, and politician. He also constructed a list of related jobs. Orator was at the top of that list, followed by jobs in banking, real estate, trust companies, and the Department of Justice. MSS1117 Malcolm X Papers, Charles H. Wright Museum of African American History.
5. Malcolm X made the statement in a speech titled "The Ballot or Bullet" given at the Audubon Ballroom in Washington Heights, New York, New York on March 29, 1964. See www.youtube.com/watch?v=ffqVJWP5OeU (accessed 6/26/17). The

address was given three days after he had encountered and been photographed with Martin Luther King, Jr. in Washington, DC. The more elaborate and more famous version of "The Ballot or the Bullet" was delivered on April 3, 1964, at Cory Methodist Church in Cleveland. The published version of that speech does not contain the phrase. It is possible that Malcolm X adapted the phrase from Cole Porter's (1934) song "Anything Goes," written for his musical of the same title. The song begins, "Times have changed/And we've often rewound the clock/Since the Puritans got a shock/When they landed on Plymouth Rock/If today/Any shock they should try to stem/'Stead of landing on Plymouth Rock/Plymouth Rock would land on them." Frank Sinatra, Ella Fitzgerald, and Tony Bennett, among others, recorded the song in the 1950s.

6. The twenty-four-year-old Prosser intended to launch his rebellion near Richmond, Virginia, on August 30, but inclement weather caused him to change plans. Before he could reorganize, two slaves betrayed him. Prosser escaped immediate capture but eventually was tracked down in Norfolk by authorities, after being betrayed again. He and twenty-five followers, including his brothers Solomon and Martin, were hanged. In the aftermath, the Virginia Assembly increased restrictions on the movements of slaves and free Blacks.

7. Newman (1998) wisely favors a variety of intentions. He agrees that the spirituals are essentially religious songs but also acknowledges that their political aspect is perhaps most important (pp. 23–4). Appropriately, he divided his collection of the spirituals in four categories: songs of faith, songs of freedom, songs of hope, and songs of the spirit.

8. The debate has been intense at least as far back as the time of the Harlem Renaissance. Intellectuals like Alain Locke in "The New Negro" (1925, p. 4) claimed the spirituals to be a unique African-American contribution, while a line of White critics, exemplified by musicologist George Pullen Jackson (1932) have considered the spirituals to be mere imitations of white folk hymnody. The most compelling scholarship, says Southern (1997), supports Locke's view.

3 Jeremiads and Manifestoes

Imperio in Imperium by Sutton Griggs, published in 1899, is perhaps the classic "rhetoric novel" in African-American literature given its high degree of self-reflexivity about the role of rhetoric and oratory in social movements. Moreover, rhetoric and oratorical contests are central to the plot. More than one-fourth of the novel consists of orations, comments about orations, letters, and written resolutions as friends and rivals Belton Piedmont and Bernard Belgrave strive to enact their educational and political visions.

Opening in northwestern Virginia during the early stages of Reconstruction, the story reveals that eight-year-old Belton begins school with unbridled enthusiasm and determination despite the fact that his white teacher regards him with disdain. Belton is poor, ragged, and dark-complexioned. His counterpart Bernard, a year older, is a financially privileged mulatto of mysterious circumstances. Not surprisingly, he is the teacher's pet. However, both boys excel and become over the course of twelve years the two best students in the school. They study rhetoric formally and develop widespread reputations as "brilliant students and eloquent speakers" (1899/2003, p. 25). Griggs even depicts them as "oratorical gladiators" (p. 27). As part of commencement exercises, the two engage in a public-speaking contest. Foreshadowing their ultimate political commitments, Belton speaks on the contributions of Anglo-Saxons to liberty while Bernard holds forth on Robert Emmett, the Irish nationalist and noted orator who was executed for leading a rebellion against British rule. By consensus, Belton is the better performer, but the gold medal is given to Bernard, leaving Belton an "uncrowned king" (p. 10).

Fortuitously, Belton soon meets a real King, a newspaper editor named V. M. King, who agrees to sponsor his education at Stowe University in Nashville. In return, King asks only that Belton always appeal to the good side of people's character (pp. 37–8). Belton manages to do so despite numerous and sometimes harrowing travails, and he matures to become the epitome of the New Negro, a confident and assertive "race man" and advocate for equal rights.[1]

In the meantime, the more privileged Bernard is shuffled off to Harvard University, where he becomes class president and valedictorian. Upon graduation, he discovers that he is the son of a United States senator and grandson of a governor. In addition, he is heir to a vast fortune. However, his father, who had summoned him, instructs him that all of this news is to remain secret, even the fact of his father's legal marriage to Bernard's mother. Following his father's wishes, he settles into life as an attorney and aspiring politician in Norfolk. He reunites with Belton when he has to defend his old schoolmate in a case that reached the Supreme Court. His speech before the magistrates was considered the best since the days of Daniel Webster (p. 108).

But Bernard's life begins to unravel. His dark-brown girlfriend Viola Martin accepts the claims of John H. Van Evrie, author of *White Supremacy and Negro Subordination* (1868), that mulattoes are abnormal and lead to the extermination of the Negro race.[2] Therefore, despite her love, she rejects Bernard. In her suicide note, she instructs him to read the book to gauge the worth of its arguments, though she took her own life before allowing the brilliant orator an opportunity to convince her that the book had no merit. Once she fell too deeply into despair, she closed the path to rational persuasion. She wrote to Bernard concerning the races, "Do not let them intermingle. Erect moral barriers to separate them. If you fail in this, make the separation physical; lead our people forth from this accursed land. Do this and I shall not have died in vain" (p. 119).

While in mourning, Bernard receives a cryptic message from Belton summoning him to Texas. After arriving and unsuspectingly passing an initiation, he is offered the presidency of the Imperium, a secret black government, co-founded by Belton, which is headquartered just outside of Waco. Belton serves as Speaker of Congress.

Bernard promptly steers the Imperium in a more militant direction and, reminiscent of Robert Emmett, eventually argues at length for a violent separation from the United States (pp. 140–9). Belton, ever true to his benefactor King, is the lone dissenter in Congress and responds with a stunning oration that turns the tide of opinion back toward peaceable adjustment (pp. 153–65). He proposes to make the Imperium public and ramp up campaigns of moral suasion. If, after four years, the federal government remained weak-willed regarding civil rights, then Belton would urge all Blacks to move to Texas and take over the state government through voting and peacefully work out their destiny as a distinct race in America. Once again, Belton wins but loses. Congress adopts his proposals, but then Bernard strikes a backroom deal with key leaders and gains approval for a war plan. At this point, Belton resigns from the Imperium, an action that carries a mandatory death penalty. After Belton's demise, Berl Trout, Secretary of State, gets to apply the final rhetorical flourish. He honors Belton's legacy and, at the price of his own death, betrays the Imperium in a letter to the general public.

In this tale of great oratorical contests, Griggs artfully dramatizes the central historical tension in African-American rhetoric. As Harold Cruse noted in *The Crisis of the Negro Intellectual* (1967/1984), African Americans have always oscillated between the integrationist strain and the separatist strain. These swings have occurred in groups and even in individuals.

Integration

The most celebrated rhetorical expression of the integrationist strain has been through the *African-American jeremiad*.[3] The term derives from the Hebrew prophet Jeremiah, who warned against straying from the Mosaic covenant and foretold the fall of Judah to the Babylonians and the destruction of the temple in Jerusalem. Such laments and predictions of calamity became known as jeremiads and were often illustrated in the American context by Puritan ministers, who warned congregations of the peril that would follow if people violated or continued to violate religious and social ideals. This *American jeremiad* resonated powerfully with the Puritan rank and file, which viewed itself as a chosen people in the New Israel, the rightful occupants of the "shining city on the hill,"[4] their place providentially sanctioned, they felt, by victory in the American Revolutionary War. The admonishments to keep worshippers on the proper moral path consisted typically of three parts:

1. the citing of the *promise*
2. criticism of *declension* or retrogression from the promise
3. a resolving *prophecy* that society will shortly complete its mission and redeem the promise.

(Howard-Pitney, 1990, p. 8)

As the prophet Jeremiah projected a positive long-term view, so did Puritan exhorters, though they also held out the prospect that the society would face doom if the promise were not redeemed.

The African-American jeremiad is an astute variation. Given their circumstances, including their exposure to evangelical Protestantism, many Blacks, however much they suffered, began to view themselves as a chosen people as well. After all, the story of Exodus was a much closer match to their reality of bondage and subjugation than to the lives of White people. They saw themselves as the Israelites, and they saw freedom both as the Promised Land and as their destiny. Within the parameters of the American Jeremiad, the nation's archetypal myth, they considered themselves to be the chosen redeemers whom America had to acknowledge properly if it were to live up to the ideal of liberty for all. When given opportunities to air grievances publicly, they drew tremendous rhetorical force from the national backsliding on the question of social equality. As a supposedly chosen people in the midst of a larger group of people also deemed chosen, Black writers and orators addressed two audiences, the Black community and the country surrounding it, whose fates were woven together.

Parts of David Walker's *Appeal* (1829/1965) powerfully exemplified the approach. Walker spoke to divine promise and to American moral deterioration:

> God, through his instrument Moses, handed a dispensation of his Divine will, to the children of Israel after they had left Egypt for the land of Canaan or of Promise, who through hypocrisy, oppression and unbelief,

departed from the faith.—He then, by his apostles, handed a dispensation of his, together with the will of Jesus Christ, to the Europeans in Europe, who, in open violation of which, have made *merchandise* of us, and it does appear as though they take this very dispensation to aid them in their *infernal* depredations upon us. Indeed, the way in which religion was and is conducted by the Europeans and their descendants, one might believe it was a plan fabricated by themselves and the *devils* to *oppress* us. But hark! My master has taught me better than to believe it—he has taught me that his gospel as it was preached by himself and his apostles remains the same, notwithstanding Europe has tried to mingle blood and oppression with it.

(p. 35)

Walker proceeded to pillory the ruling elites and their representatives in the ministry, and he forecast retribution for the implementation and maintenance of slavery:

What the American preachers can think of us, I aver this day before God, I have never been able to define. They have newspapers and monthly periodicals, which they receive in continual succession, but on the pages of which, you will scarcely ever find a paragraph respecting slavery, which is ten thousand times more injurious to this country than all the other evils put together; and which will be the final overthrow of its government, unless something is very speedily done; for their cup is nearly full.—Perhaps they will laugh and make light of this; but I tell you Americans! That unless you speedily alter your course, you and your *Country are gone!!!!!!* For God Almighty will tear up the face of the earth*!!!*

(p. 39)

Walker's prophecy, which merged the African-American jeremiad with Ethiopianism's Decline of the West theme, came to pass. Or at least that is one conclusion that can be drawn from the epochal upheaval known as the American Civil War. The institution of slavery was eliminated and *the country as it was known was gone*, an action accompanied by much landscape destruction. A number of other Black orators and writers also predicted this turn of events, including Frederick Douglass, who fulminated after the election in 1848 of slaveholding Zachary Taylor to be the twelfth president of the United States. Rallying abolitionist forces, he presaged,

Slavery will be attacked in its stronghold—the compromises of the Constitution, and the cry of disunion shall be more fearlessly proclaimed, till slavery be abolished, the Union dissolved, or the sun of this guilty nation must go down in blood.

(1848/1950, p. 347)

Although slavery ended, racism has endured. Thus, Black advocates who have expressed optimism about creating a more perfect, multicultural democracy have produced memorable jeremiads through post-Reconstruction (Griggs's character Belton Piedmont), the Progressive Era, the New Deal, the New Frontier, and beyond. For example, W.E.B. Du Bois, addressing the Niagara convention in 1906, held on to the American promise and the notion of entwined racial and ethnic fates while delivering critique:

> We claim for ourselves every single right that belongs to a freeborn American, political civil and social; and until we get these rights we will never cease to protest and assail the ears of America. The battle we wage is not for ourselves alone but for all true Americans. It is a fight for ideals, lest this, our common fatherland, false to its founding, become in truth the land of the thief and the home of the Slave—a byword and a hissing among the nations for its sounding pretentions and pitiful accomplishment.
>
> (1906/1996, p. 374)

This penchant for the African-American jeremiad was typical of Du Bois over the first third of the twentieth century. When he supported the idea of African-American soldiers fighting in World War I, he argued, "We Americans, black and white, are the servants of all mankind and ministering to a greater, fairer heaven. Let us be true to our mission. No land that loves to lynch 'niggers' can lead the hosts of Almighty God" (1917/1996, p. 379).

During the administration of President Franklin Delano Roosevelt, a member of his "Black Cabinet,"[5] Mary McLeod Bethune, made rhetorical use of the American promise in her essay "Certain Unalienable Rights":

> What, then, does the Negro want? His answer is very simple. He wants only what all other Americans want. He wants opportunity to make real what the Declaration of Independence and the Constitution and Bill of Rights say; what the Four Freedoms[6] establish. While he knows these ideals are open to no man completely he wants only his equal chance to attain them. . . . This is all that the Negro asks. He will not willingly accept less. As long as America offers less, she will be that much less a democracy. The whole way is the American way.
>
> (pp. 253–5)

Bethune did not present a fully formed jeremiad and speak stridently either to triumph or calamity. Perhaps she felt constrained by her status as an "official" or as a woman not expected to address forcefully a general readership.

Such constriction was not an issue for Martin Luther King, Jr. at the March on Washington, where he delivered "I Have a Dream," the most famous African-American jeremiad. Using the classic structure, King addressed the American covenant:

> In a sense we've come to our nation's capital to cash a check. When the architects of our republic wrote the magnificent words of the Constitution

and the Declaration of Independence, they were signing a promissory note to which every American was to fall heir. This note was the promise that all men, yes, black men as well as white men, would be guaranteed the unalienable rights of life, liberty, and the pursuit of happiness.

(p. 217)

King contrasted this vision to the nation's shortcomings, its declension. He declared:

> It is obvious today that America has defaulted on this promissory note in so far as her citizens of color are concerned. Instead of honoring this sacred obligation, America has given the Negro people a bad check; a check which has come back marked "insufficient funds."

(p. 217)

Then, correctly predicting the long, hot summers to come, King contended:

> the whirlwinds of revolt will continue to shake the foundations of our nation until the bright day of justice emerges.

(p. 218)

However, in the fashion of a true jeremiad, the forecast is contingent—until. In fact, King expressed faith that the bright day of justice eventually *will* emerge:

> we will be able to transform the jangling discords of our nation into a beautiful symphony of brotherhood.

(p. 219)

Moreover, he had indicated, as is characteristic of African-American jeremiads, that he was conscious of addressing a double audience; his vision of Black progress was a "dream deeply rooted in the American dream" (p. 219).

Perhaps the most notable recent example of the African-American jeremiad is Michelle Alexander's best-selling *The New Jim Crow* (2012). The book is tied firmly to King's vision, particularly his late-1960s calls for radical transformations in American society.[7] As Alexander articulates,

> We should hope not for a colorblind society but instead for a world in which we can see each other fully, learn from each other, and do what we can to respond to each other with love. That was King's dream—a society that is capable of seeing each of us, as we are, with love. That is a goal worth fighting for.

(p. 244)

Although textually not hugging the American promise as firmly as King did, Alexander, a civil rights attorney, suggests by extension her support for the ideal of an egalitarian democracy that was entwined with the nation's founding. However, she also understands the moral failings of the Founding Fathers, who in their political compromises promoted inequities, including legal slavery. This began the long declension that has produced three racial caste systems over the course of American history, namely, slavery, Jim Crow, and mass incarceration. The primary imperatives, as Alexander explains, have been exploitation in the case of slavery, subordination during the era of Jim Crow, and marginalization in the present carceral state or, as it is sometimes referred to, the prison-industrial complex (p. 219). The complexion of the exploding jail population is overwhelmingly black and brown. Therefore, Alexander asserts, "We have not ended racial caste in America; we have merely redesigned it" (p. 1). She declares, as well, "a human rights nightmare is occurring on our watch" (p. 15).

This is the New Jim Crow. This is the system, undergirded by a so-called War on Drugs, by which the penal population has increased sevenfold over the past 30 years and now stands at more than 2 million (p. 93). The increase, Alexander informs us, is attributable mostly to policy changes and racial disparities regarding arrests, prosecutions, and sentencing. Crime rates have not increased, and the rate of drug use is similar across the American racial spectrum (p. 93, p. 7). Essential to comprehend, according to Alexander, is that mass incarceration is a "comprehensive well-disguised system of racialized social control" and incorporates, beyond the immediate confines of the criminal justice apparatus, the larger network of rules, policies, laws, and customs that restrict possibility for those labeled criminals and consign them to a "hidden underworld of legalized discrimination and permanent social exclusion" (p. 13).

Along with gesturing to American promise and painstakingly detailing American shortcomings, Alexander employs the discourse of crisis, which one would expect in a jeremiad. She speaks about a "crisis faced by communities of color" and of the "enormity of the crisis at hand" (p. 11). She does not provide the hell-and-damnation fervor of a Puritan preacher or David Walker, yet she does posit a doomsday scenario:

> While marginalization may sound far preferable to exploitation, it may prove to be even more dangerous. Extreme marginalization, as we have seen throughout world history, poses the risk of extermination. Tragedies such as the Holocaust in Germany or ethnic cleansing in Bosnia are traceable to the extreme marginalization and stigmatization of racial and ethnic groups.
> (p. 219)

Moreover, given that no racial caste system has been unaccompanied by revolt, the specter of the "whirlwinds" that King mentioned is invoked. Or as Alexander puts the matter, aware of the turbulent national history relative to racial advancement:

> A civil war had to be waged to end slavery; a mass movement was necessary to bring a formal end to Jim Crow. Those who imagine that far less is

required to dismantle mass incarceration and build a new egalitarian racial consensus reflecting a compassionate rather than punitive impulse toward poor people of color fail to appreciate the distance between Martin Luther King Jr.'s dream and the ongoing racial nightmare for those locked up and locked out of American society.

(p. 235)

King, in fact, is the hero of Alexander's final chapter. She mentions or cites him at least 15 times over the book's closing 35 pages, and she conveys his sense of "the fierce urgency of now," even quoting the phrase, which is one of the verbal gems from "I Have a Dream" (King, pp. 217–18). Although she does not exactly repeat his certainty about progress, she does align herself as closely as she can with his prophecy and provides an update:

> If Martin Luther King Jr. is right that the arc of history is long, but it bends toward justice, a new movement will arise; and if civil rights organizations fail to keep up with the times, they will be pushed to the side as another generation of advocates comes to the fore. Hopefully the new generation will be led by those who know best the brutality of the new caste system—a group with greater vision, courage, and determination than the old guard can muster, trapped as they may be in an outdated paradigm. This new generation of activists should not disrespect their elders or disparage their contributions or achieve-ments; to the contrary, they should bow their heads in respect, for their forerunners have expended untold hours and made great sacrifices in an elusive quest for justice. But once respects have been paid, they should march right past them, emboldened, as King once said, by the "fierce urgency of now."

(p. 260)

With a full rhetorical embrace of King and a closing nod to James Baldwin's *The Fire Next Time* (1963), Alexander stirringly concludes her latter-day, African-American jeremiad.

Separatism

In his 1897 essay "The Conservation of Races," Du Bois sketched a classic conundrum:

> Here, then, is the dilemma, and is a puzzling one, I admit. No Negro who has given earnest thought to the situation of his people in America has failed to ask himself at some time: What, after all, am I? Am I an American or am I a Negro? Can I be both? Or is it my duty to cease to be a Negro as soon as possible and be an American? If I strive as a Negro, am I not

perpetuating the very cleft that threatens and separates Black and White America? Is not my only possible practical aim the subduction of all that is Negro in me to the American? Does my black blood place upon me any more obligation to assert my nationality than German, or Irish or Italian blood would?

(1897/1996, p. 43)

Du Bois revisited this series of questions and lived its tension through much of his long life. Although at times the exemplary African-American Jeremiah and a standard-bearer of the integrationist NAACP, he also favored a number of Black-nationalist initiatives and was even dubbed the Father of Pan-Africanism for his efforts to connect African-American political aspirations and activities to those of Black Africans and Black African-descended people the world over.

Du Bois's fluctuations or multiple outlooks suggest, along with genuine existential grappling, varying degrees of optimism/pessimism regarding the prospect of social justice for Blacks within mainstream American society. On many occasions, like the character Bernard Belgrave, he would stress Black cultural and historical specificity over an integrationist ideal, though always without the demand for a separate nation-state. He would not agree with his contemporary and unapologetic Black separatist, Marcus Garvey.

In "Africa for the Africans," Garvey (1923/1986) explained the political direction of the Universal Negro Improvement Association (UNIA), the organization that he founded and headed. He included thinly disguised criticism of Du Bois, one of his most famous adversaries:

> For five years the Universal Negro Improvement Association has been advocating the cause of Africa for Africans—that is, that the Negro peoples of the world should concentrate upon the object of building up for themselves a great nation in Africa.
>
> When we started our propaganda toward this end several of the so-called intellectual Negroes who have been bamboozling the race for over half a century said that we were crazy, that the Negro peoples of the western world were not interested in Africa and could not live in Africa. One editor and leader went so far as to say at his so-called Pan-African Congress that American Negroes were not interested in Africa and could not live in Africa, because the climate was too hot. All kinds of arguments have been adduced by these Negro intellectuals against the colonization of Africa by the black race. Some said that the black man would ultimately work out his existence alongside of the white man in countries founded and established by the latter. Therefore, it was not necessary for Negroes to seek an independent nationality on their own. The old time stories of "African fever," "African bad climate," "African mesquitos," "African savages," have been repeated by these "brainless intellectuals" of ours as a scare against our people in America and the West Indies taking a kindly

interest in the new program of building a racial empire of our own in our Motherland.

(p. 68)

Pressing home his perspective, Garvey argued that, despite what in his view were misguided attacks against him and his work, "the time has really come for the Asiatics to govern themselves in Asia, as the Europeans are in Europe and the Western world, so also is it wise for the Africans to govern themselves at home and thereby bring peace and satisfaction to the entire human family" (p. 72).

Garvey's influence was widespread and reached three people who would profoundly affect Malcolm X. Malcolm's parents, Earl Little and Louise Little, were both followers of Garvey during Malcolm's early childhood. Elijah Muhammad, founder and leader of the Nation of Islam and the primary mentor to Malcolm over most of Malcolm's public career, also was influenced by the UNIA. He later led the Nation of Islam for more than forty years. Although the organization sought social justice and equality of opportunity, its most provocative political prescription for the advancement of African Americans on the whole was separatism. Muhammad presented this position numerous times over the decades, including in *Message to the Blackman* (1973):

> We want our people in America whose parents or grandparents were descendants from slaves to be allowed, to establish a separate state or territory of their own—either on this continent or elsewhere. We believe that our former slave-masters are obligated to maintain and supply our needs in this separate territory for the next 20 or 25 years until we are able to produce and supply our own needs.
>
> Since we cannot get along with them in peace and equality after giving them 400 years of our sweat and blood and receiving in return some of the worst treatment human beings have ever experienced, we believe our contributions to this land and the suffering force upon us by white America justifies our demand for complete separation in a state or territory of our own.

(p. 161)

Muhammad understood that some Blacks might reject the proposal, but he argued that every Black man and woman should have the option to accept separatism (p. 162). He contended furthermore that offers of integration were deceptive and designed to prevent Blacks from realizing that separatism was appropriate for the times (pp. 163–4). As national spokesman for the Nation of Islam, Malcolm promoted Muhammad's brand of nationalism, repeatedly detailing Muhammad's plan, which called for the federal government to sponsor relocation and provide start-up financing, materials, and technology until Blacks established themselves as a nation independent of whites.

After leaving the Nation of Islam in early 1964, Malcolm espoused a more nuanced revolutionary ideology. Black nationalism then meant to him, as expressed in his speech "The Ballot or the Bullet," community control of political activities, economic operations, and social/cultural initiatives. Moreover, he announced a willingness to engage in political, economic, social, and civic activism with anybody concerned with eliminating the hardships experienced by the Black community. Although not explicitly separatist, his speech is *not* about reforming white people or buying into the notion of America as a morally wayward country struggling toward redemption:

> So I say, in spreading a gospel such as black nationalism, it is not designed to make the black man re-evaluate the white man—you know him already—but to make the black man re-evaluate himself. Don't change the white man's mind—you can't change his mind, and that whole thing about appealing to the moral conscience of America—America's conscience is bankrupt. She lost all conscience long time ago. Uncle Sam has no conscience. They don't know what morals are. They don't try to eliminate an evil because it's evil, or because it's immoral; they eliminate it only when it threatens their existence. So you're wasting your time appealing to the moral conscience of a bankrupt man like Uncle Sam. If he had a conscience, he'd straighten this thing out with no more pressure being put upon him. So it is not necessary to change the white man's mind. We have to change our own mind. You can't change his mind about us. We've got to change our own minds about each other. We have to see each other with new eyes. We have to see each other as brothers and sisters. We have to come together with warmth so we can develop unity and harmony that's necessary to get this problem solved ourselves.
>
> (1965b, pp. 39–40)

Malcolm, at least that version of Malcolm, still would not choose Belton Piedmont over Bernard Belgrave. Neither would he second, say, Mary McLeod Bethune's contention that the whole way is the American way. He viewed the arc of American history differently.

Black Power

Black-nationalist thought flourished in the post-Malcolm era, especially among young people who agreed with ideas about militant assertion and self-determination. The clarion call "Black Power" marked the period more than any other exhortation. A term used by the likes of Richard Wright and Adam Clayton Powell, Jr. in earlier decades, "Black Power" became an extremely effective slogan when Willie Ricks and Stokely Carmichael reinvigorated the term in June 1966 during the Meredith March in Mississippi, a procession coordinated in part by King's Southern Christian Leadership Conference (SCLC).[8] Although by several reports, it was Ricks who first comprehensively understood the rhetorical value, the mass appeal, of the Black Power slogan in the 1960s, Student Nonviolent Coordinating Committee leader Carmichael became the national symbol of Black Power after speaking at a rally of 600 people in Greenwood upon his release from jail.[9] Cleveland Sellers, a fellow activist, provided the following account:

> *Realizing that he was in his element, with his people, Stokely let it all hang out.* "This is the twenty-seventh time I have been arrested—and I ain't going to jail no more!" *The crowd exploded into cheers and clapping.*
>
> The only way we gonna stop them white men from whuppin' us is to take over. We been saying freedom for six years and we ain't got nothin'. What we gonna start saying now is Black Power!"
>
> *The crowd was right with him. They picked up his thoughts immediately.*
>
> "BLACK POWER" *they roared in unison.*
>
> *Willie Ricks, who is as good at orchestrating the emotions of a crowd as anyone I have ever seen, sprang into action. Jumping to the platform with Stokely, he yelled to the crowd,* "What do you want?"
>
> "BLACK POWER!"
>
> "What do you want?"
>
> "BLACK POWER!"
>
> "What do you want?"
>
> "BLACK POWER!! BLACK POWER!!! BLACK POWER!!!!"
>
> (Carmichael, 2003, p. 507)

Under the deft orchestration of Ricks, who had used the term at earlier gatherings, a memorable rhetorical gauntlet had been flamboyantly thrown down inside the mainstream Civil Rights Movement.[10]

The next evening, SCLC official Hosea Williams tried to rouse the crowd with chants of "Freedom Now." But the sound meter favored the Black Powerists. This is not to say that Black Power became the dominant form of black political engagement. A large analysis of community engagement, political protest, institution building, union organizing, and boycott campaigns is beyond the scope of this book. What we are specifying is that the terms of debate *within* the mainstream Civil Rights Movement had been shifted. Never again would the Civil Rights Movement be discussed only with reference to terms like "Freedom Now" or "We Shall Overcome." Indeed, only two days after the Carmichael speech in Greenwood, King himself was forced to discuss Black Power as he walked alongside Carmichael through the Mississippi Delta (Branch, 2006, p. 487).

One of the beauties of the catchphrase was its expansive reach. If it meant flexing Black voting muscle, as Carmichael indicated to an accompanying reporter, then King could hardly object. After all, that's what much of the marching was about. But King felt compelled to interject a dissenting comment: "It would be difficult for me to use the phrase black power because of the connotative meaning that it has for many people" (Branch, 2006, p. 487).

King, of course, was always wary of the specter of Black retaliatory violence and of armed struggle, which could also be signified by the cry of Black Power. So his first-blush response was predictable. But most likely his mental gears were already spinning about how best to engage a slogan he already knew he could not suppress. SNCC already rivaled King's popularity in circles of youthful Black activism. If he came out in strident opposition to Black Power, this vibrant expression of militant Black ethos, he risked a crucial setback in terms of trying to extend his influence among young, radically inclined African Americans. King also knew that the rhetorical contest was vital because perception counted as much, if not more, than detailed substance. After all, Carmichael was not developing any more radical political platform than King was. For example, Carmichael's book *Black Power*, co-authored with Charles Hamilton and published in 1967, is no more to the left than King's *Where Do We Go From Here?* (1968), a book that was written at virtually the same time. In fact, King's move leftward was shrinking his audience in white America. If he couldn't improve his approval ratings among young Blacks, a group with whom SCLC needed to continue to recruit and work with, he at least had to halt a slide that could become irreversible. So he had to engage the Black Power slogan productively—and swiftly. This was another case of the "fierce urgency of now."

Indeed, Black-Power discourse moved at a runaway pace. Speaking at the annual convention of the NAACP less than three weeks after the Greenwood rally, executive secretary Roy Wilkins unequivocally denounced the idea of Black Power. No matter how the concept is spun, Wilkins reasoned, it denoted "anti-white power" (1966/1969, p. 91). He acknowledged that "Black Power" might provide a psychological boost to frustrated, deprived, persecuted, and frustrated black people, but he ultimately judged the idea to be "a reverse Mississippi, a reverse Hitler, a reverse Ku Klux Klan," and he vowed that, concerning the NAACP, "it shall not now poison our forward march" (pp. 91–2).

The analysis of Wilkins was obviously flawed in terms of his assessment of what Black Power could mean with respect to practical politics. Furthermore, he underplayed the value of being lifted psychologically. But Wilkins said what most NAACPers at the convention, as well as much of mainstream America, wanted to hear. This included vice president Hubert Humphrey (1966/1969), who at the same convention condemned Black Power almost precisely as Wilkins had done the day before.

On September 22, 1966, Carmichael published "What We Want" in the *New York Review of Books*. The piece addressed the recent battle over ideas, which, as we know, was also a battle about language:

> An organization which claims to speak for the needs of a community—as does the Student Nonviolent Coordinating Committee—must speak in the tone of that community, not as someone else's buffer zone. This is the significance of black power as a slogan. For once, black people are going to use the words they want to use—not just the words whites want to hear.

And they will do this no matter how often the press tries to stop the use of the slogan by equating it with racism or separatism.

An organization which claims to be working for the needs of a community—as SNCC does—must work to provide that community with a position of strength from which to make its voice heard. This is the significance of black power beyond the slogan.

(p. 5)

But the issue was not settled. By the end of the fall, feature articles about Black Power had appeared in all major news outlets. The November 1966 issue of *Negro Digest* featured a print symposium titled "The Meaning and Measure of Black Power." A dozen writers and prominent figures, namely, Julian Bond, Anita Cornwell, Ronald Fair, Eloise Greenfield, Nathan Hare, Brooks Johnson, John Oliver Killens, Dudley Randall, Conrad Kent Rivers, Sterling Stuckey, Eugene Walton, and Francis Ward, offered their takes on the matter.

Meanwhile, preparations were underway for a national conference on Black Power to be held in Newark in July 1967. Floyd McKissick, who as the national director of the Congress of Racial Equality had been the third organization leader involved in the Meredith March, advocated Black Power when he addressed the gathering:

> The propaganda of white supremacy is advanced through advertising, entertainment and through education and folklore that ignores the con-tributions of Black People to World Civilization; through the acceptance of the European standard of beauty and culture, while disparaging and disregarding the values of three quarters of the world—while ignoring the beauty that is Black.
>
> How else could you explain the failure of some Black people to under-stand and accept Black Power? Any rational person or group of people understand the need for self-preservation.
>
> Could it be that some Black People have been so misled, so confused by white America that they don't understand they need power of their own to protect themselves? Could it be that some middle-class Negroes have become so enamored with the death wish of integration—the dream of absorption and disappearance into the white man's culture—that he fears his Blackness?
>
> (1967/1969, pp. 135–6)

Whatever the answer to McKissick, the point here is that over the course of little more than a year, numerous orators and writers had staked out the ideological boundaries of the discourse about Black Power. This is the con-tinuum along which King deftly worked. While he never embraced the Black Power slogan (one end), he was never simplistically antagonistic toward it (the other end).

As we have noted, King carefully considered Black Power's premises and rhetorical effects. This means, among other things, that he took Carmichael, McKissick, and others seriously. Chapter 2 of *Where Do Go from Here?* is titled "Black Power." At forty-four pages, it is by far the longest chapter in the book. He reminded us early on about his sensitivity to language as he recalled a five-hour conversation he participated in with members of the Southern Christian Leadership Conference, the Congress of Racial Equality, and the Student Non-violent Coordinating Committee. His recollection is worth quoting at length because it illustrates debaters engaging one another directly in a process of deliberation:

> For five long hours I pleaded with the group to abandon the Black power slogan. It was my contention that a leader has to be concerned about the problem of semantics. Each word, I said, has a denotative meaning—its explicit and recognized sense—and a connotative meaning—its suggestive sense. While the concept of legitimate "Black Power" might be denotatively sound, the slogan "Black Power" carried the wrong connotation. I mentioned the implications of violence that the press had already attached to the phrase. And I went on to say that some of the rash statements on the part of a few marchers only reinforced this impression.
>
> Stokely replied by saying that the question of violence versus nonviolence was irrelevant. That the real question was the need for black people to consolidate their political and economic resources to achieve power. "Power," he said, "is the only thing respected in the world, and we must get it at any cost." Then he looked me squarely in the eye and said, "Martin, you know as well as I do that practically every other ethnic group in America has done just this. The Jews, the Irish and Italians did it, why can't we?"
>
> "That is just the point," I answered. "No one has ever heard the Jews publicly chant a slogan Jewish power, but they have power. Through group unity, determination and creative endeavor, they have gained it. The same is true of Irish and Italians. Neither group has used a slogan of Irish or Italian power, but they have worked hard to achieve it. This is exactly what we must do," I said. We must use every constructive means to amass economic and political power. This is the kind of legitimate power we need. We must work to build racial pride and refute the notion that black is evil and ugly. But this must come through a program, not merely through a slogan.
>
> Stokely and Floyd insisted that the slogan itself was important. "How can you arouse people to unite around a program without a slogan as a rallying cry? Didn't the labor movement have slogans? Haven't we had slogans all along in the freedom movement? What we need is a new slogan with 'black' in it."
>
> I conceded the fact that we must have slogans. But why have one that would confuse our allies, isolate the Negro community and give many

prejudiced whites, who might otherwise be ashamed of their anti-Negro feeling, a ready excuse for self-justification?

"Why not use the slogan 'black consciousness' or 'black equality'?" I suggested. "These phrases would be less vulnerable and would more accurately describe what we are about. The words 'black' and 'power' together give the impression that we are talking about black domination rather than black equality."

Stokely responded that neither would have the ready appeal and persuasive force of Black Power. Throughout the lengthy discussion, Stokely and Floyd remained adamant, and Stokely concluded by saying, with candor, "Martin, I deliberately decided to raise this issue on the march in order to give it a national forum, and force you to take a stand for Black power."

I laughed. "I have been used before,'" I said to Stokely. "One more time won't hurt."

(1968, pp. 30–1)

King never would adopt separatist implications or suggestions of retaliatory violence. Moreover, he had turned by that time more toward the economic front and preferred a clarion call of "Power for Poor People" rather than one of "Black Power." Yet he spent pages upon pages explaining the disappointment and disenchantment that led to the cry of "Black Power" in the first place. It was a smart move. Without resorting to ridicule or flat opposition, he rearticulated the discourses of Black Power within his larger progressive vision. It was not a co-opting maneuver; he gained precious little, if anything, for it in material terms. But it was a move that helped to bring coherence to his later, radical jeremiad and, thus, to his radical legacy. If the Stokely Carmichaels and Floyd McKissicks of the world wanted Black Power, they surely could have had no objection to securing it within the context of King's imagined world house.

Of course, Black Power and Black Nationalism more broadly resonate with many today. Only full freedom, justice, and equality could prevent such occurrence. For now, pundits and other worried observers monitor websites to see if those sites explicitly promote violence toward authorities. And without a doubt, we can hear the echoes of Wilkins's ridiculing of Black Power every time one person presses somebody else to reject the slogan "Black Lives Matter."

Notes

1. According to Gates (1988b), in "The Trope of a New Negro and the Reconstruction of the Image of the Black," *New Negro* is a locution that generally described African Americans who were politically and culturally assertive in trying to move beyond the bounds of enslavement and Jim Crow, and the expression is traceable to the 1890s and became most popular during the Harlem Renaissance, also known as the New Negro Renaissance. A *race man* or *race woman* is generally regarded as an African American who stands and agitates for the rights of African Americans.

2. Van Evrie claimed his work demonstrated that "even when both white and negro become so debauched, degraded, and sinful as to equalize and harmonize together,

as we see with Portugese and Spaniards on this Continent, and sometimes with individuals among ourselves, who mate and mix their blood, their progeny become sterile, diseased, rotten, and within a certain time, utterly perish from the earth" (1868, p. vi.) He elaborates on this idea in the chapter titled "Mulattoism and Mongrelism" (pp. 143–67).

3. I use the term *African-American jeremiad* as a spin on Howard-Pitney's title, *The Afro-American Jeremiad: Appeals for Justice in America* (1990). Howard-Pitney coined his term partly in response to Wilson Moses (1982), who used the phrase *Black jeremiad* in *Black Messiahs and Uncle Toms: Social and Literary Manipulations of a Religious Myth* (pp. 30–1).

4. The phrase is drawn from the Sermon on the Mount (Matthew 5:14): "You are the light of the world. A city that is set on a hill cannot be hidden." Scholars often point to John Winthrop (1630, "A Model of Christian Charity") as the first person to employ the term in the colonies. The saying has become of a staple of American political discourse. On June 8, 2017, FBI director James Comey, testifying before the Senate Intelligence Committee, summarized the standing of the United States as, "We are still that shining city on the hill."

5. Not an official designation, the Black Cabinet was an informal network of policy advisors to President Franklin Delano Roosevelt and first lady Eleanor Roosevelt. Members included Mary McLeod Bethune, Rayford Logan, and Robert C. Weaver.

6. In the 1941 State of the Union address, President Roosevelt defined the four freedoms as freedom of speech, freedom of worship, freedom from want, and freedom from fear.

7. In *Where Do We Go from Here?* (1968), King wrote, "there is need for a radical restructuring of the architecture of American society. For its very survival's sake, America must re-examine old presuppositions and release itself from many things that for centuries have been held sacred. For the evils of racism, poverty and militarism to die, a new set of values must be born. Our economy must become more person-centered than property-and profit-centered. Our government must depend more on its moral power than on its military power. Let us, therefore, not think of our movement as one that seeks to integrate the Negro into all the existing values of American society. Let us be those creative dissenters who will call our beloved nation to a higher destiny, to a new plateau of compassion, to a more noble expression of humaneness" (p. 133). King proposed a guaranteed income (pp. 162–6) and brought a progressive perspective to issues of education, employment, rights, and housing (pp. 193–202).

8. The Congress on Racial Equality (CORE) and the Student Nonviolent Coordinating Committee (SNCC) sponsored the march along with the Southern Christian Leadership Conference (SCLC).

9. See Carmichael (2003, pp. 507–8) and Branch (2006, pp. 485–7).

10. Branch (2006) provides a variation of Carmichael's speech (p. 486): "This the 27th time I have been arrested," he began, "and I ain't going to jail no more!" He said Negroes should stay home from Vietnam and fight for black power in Greenwood. "We want black power!" he shouted five times, jabbing his forefinger downward in the air. "That's right. That's what we want, black power. We don't have to be ashamed of it. We have stayed here. We have begged the president. We've begged the federal government—that's all we've been doing, begging and begging. It's time we stand up and take over. Every courthouse in Mississippi ought to be burned down tomorrow to get rid of the dirt and the mess. From now on, when they ask you what you want, you know what to tell 'em. What do you want?"

The crowd shouted, "Black power!" Willie Ricks sprang up to help lead thunderous rounds of call and response: "What do you want?" "Black power!" (p. 486).

4   Rhetorical Theory

Increasingly, African-American rhetoric is being studied and discussed in colleges and universities. We cannot yet account for all of the ways that these activities transpire. Teaching methods vary, and course content and extracurricular conversation range across a wide discursive territory. However, it is still meaningful to outline several influential theories and theoretical gestures that circulate in academic circles about African-American rhetoric. Obviously, these are not the only strands of thinking that are relevant, but they have proven to be especially generative.

Afrocentric Ideas

Molefi Kete Asante, originally known as Arthur Lee Smith, has provided the most comprehensive scholarly discussion of African-American rhetoric. Although formal study of Black rhetoric dates back to the nineteenth century, it is Asante's work as a rhetoric scholar and cultural analyst since he earned a doctoral degree in communication studies from UCLA in 1968 that anchors the field. All serious students of African-American rhetoric who have emerged during the past five decades have had to engage his scholarship, an oeuvre that includes *Rhetoric of Black Revolution* (1969); *The Voice of Black Rhetoric* (1971); *Language, Communication, and Rhetoric in Black America* (1972); *The Afrocentric Idea* (1998); *Race, Rhetoric, and Identity* (2005); and *Lynching Barack Obama* (2016). Of these, *The Afrocentric Idea* is the most important. He declares in the introduction his commitment to the "systematic exposition of communication and cultural behaviors as they are articulated in the African world" (1998, p. xv). By *African world* he means both the continent of Africa and the diaspora. In short, he has sought to establish an analytic framework capacious enough to speak to all aspects of African-derived rhetorical culture.

Although the term *Afrocentric* conjures up for some visions of isolationism and essentialism, the actual Afrocentric rhetorical project described by Asante is quite the opposite. In his view, "rhetoric must transcend ideologies, whether political or racial, in order to perform the task of continuous reconciliation" (p. 183). In other words, Afrocentric rhetoric confronts and extends beyond the negations imposed by Western society in which Eurocentric ideals have often stood atop knowledge and culture hierarchies with the result that the Black difference typically has been construed as deficiency. Afrocentric rhetoric, to the contrary, promotes a humanistic vision that confirms the worth of other cultures and imagines nonhierarchical coexistence among them. It aims to unite people based on mutual recognition and respect (p. xi). As Asante phrases the matter,

> Afrocentricity's response certainly is not to impose its own particularity as a universal, as Eurocentricity has often done. But hearing the voice of African American culture with all of its attendant parts is one way of creating a more sane society and one model for a more humane world.
>
> (p. 23)

The Afrocentric conception and its practical politics are explicitly antiracist, antisexist, and anticlassist (p. 42). It is, Asante announces, the "productive thrust of language into the unknown in an attempt to create harmony and balance in the midst of disharmony and indecision" (p. 46)

Concerning the essential characteristics of Afrocentric rhetoric, Asante asserts that they are reflective of the "internal mythic clock, the epic memory, the psychic stain" of Africa in the spirits of African Americans (p. 59). This is a line that flirts with essentialism, but it is not the positing of a transhistorical, immutable, mystical essence as the explanation for a particular communicative style. Asante knows the impossibility of drawing lengthy straight lines of causation or direct connections through mazes of intertwining cultural histories. Furthermore, he grasps the nature of historical cultural diversity in Africa and the reality that history is open ended. African Americans are heirs to all traditions. But what Asante is stressing are the lived core experiences of African societies that have been passed along for centuries both on the continent and in the diaspora (p. 13). Thus, African-American culture contains African retentions. But retentions do not make it unique among cultures. Its uniqueness lies in the fact that it is African-sourced in the United States. Its essence is that it is a repository of influences of which African ones are defining. Otherwise there would be no field of African-American rhetoric for it would lack an object of study.

To consider the effects of cultural difference on rhetorical practice more closely, while keeping in mind the idea of proportions as opposed to absolutes, let us turn, as Asante occasionally does, to Aristotle's definition of rhetoric, that is, "an ability, in each [particular] case, to see the available means of persuasion" (2006, p. 37). This is still probably the most familiar definition of rhetoric among academics and students, one that indicates, Asante notes, a clear conceptual separation in the meaning-making functions of speaker and listener or writer and reader. Rather than emphasizing the audience participation and the co-creation of meaning that are more characteristic of African verbal culture with its prevalent call-and-response modality, the classic Aristotelian formulation suggests people independently manipulating "means" to persuade others through "delivery." This conception of emitter and receiver, according to Asante, is a "Euro-linear construction, situated in a stimulus-response ideology" (1998, p. 28). On the other hand, in Afrocentric rhetoric, the speaker consciously operates under guidance from the audience, and effective performance cannot be ascertained apart from audience participation or, more precisely, audience demands relative to expressions, gestures, and tone (p. 52). If Black audiences are moved to assent, they don't simply say, "We agree." They are apt to holler, "Teach!" The degree of direction is beyond something as passive as a "response." In some instances, the speaker sets in motion certain aspects of the monitoring system to co-create the message or what might be more accurately called a *message event*. Both on numerous religious and sacred occasions a speaker will exclaim, "Can I get an Amen?"

The call-and-response dynamic is so pervasive in African-American culture that one could hardly test Black verbal soil and not discover it.[1] Generations have attended soul music concerts where the entertainer asks "all the ladies" and "all the fellas" to participate in the show. Sometimes the groups are facetiously pitted against one another with the aim of making the show a more vibrant experience for all in attendance.

A classic recorded example of call-and-response is provided by old-school rapper Kurtis Blow on the magisterial "The Breaks" (1980). The recording is more than a rap song; it is a party. The sound of revelers is heard in the background throughout and some respond to Blow's serial statements of misfortunate by concurring, "That's the breaks. That's the breaks." At one point, the rapper initiates the following exchange:

> Somebody say all right.
> *all ri-ight.*
> Say Ho-o!
> *Ho-o!*
> You don't stop. Now somebody scream.

Everyone in the house does, solidifying the communication.

Later on the track, Kurtis Blow commands rhythmically, "Just do it, just do it, just do it, do it, do it!" It is not a directive because the audience is not being requested to perform any particular action. The gesture they make is to echo Kurtis Blow's cry.

A similar scenario is presented in the recent movie *Straight Outta Compton* (2015). As the Ice Cube character leads N.W.A. on a rendition of the 1998 song, "Dopeman," he declares, "Do that shit, do that shit, do it!" The audience, including the group's white manager, gets the spirit and repeats the chant. The performance also involves, as on "The Breaks," an invitation to the audience to scream, which it does. In addition, the film shows the now-familiar move of a rapper extending the microphone toward the crowd so the audience members can spit some of the lyrics.

Or consider Kirk Franklin's (1997) recording in another genre as he queries his collaborators, the gospel choir God's Property:

> GP are you wit me?
> Oh yeah. We having church; we ain't going nowhere.
> GP are you wit me?
> Oh yeah. We having church; we ain't going nowhere.
> GP are you wit me?
> Oh yeah. We having church; we ain't going nowhere.

A fine example of call-and-response in an audio (and video) recording, "Stomp" sublimely rearticulates Asante's observation that the African oral tradition features polyrhythms, talk back, hand clapping, and other affirmations as speaker and audience push toward unity (Asante, 1998, p. 59).

The call-and-response dynamic also has implications for political analysis and action. If the contrast between vertical speaker-audience manifestations and the antiphonal, horizontal quality of Afrocentric speaker-audience interaction reflects deep cultural preferences, then vertical or horizontal social relations will flourish where these respective styles predominate. At least this is an easy theoretical leap for Asante to make. Addressing the broad cultural character of rhetoric, he observes, "There are therefore speaker and listener societies—a plethora of possibilities to keep the 'oppressed' in their places and the oppressors in theirs" (p. 180). It becomes "natural," therefore, that some groups or nations should speak while others listen. This is not to argue that communicative styles determine all oppressive social arrangements, but it is to suggest that progressive movements are bound to falter to the extent that they are inattentive to the various constructions of speaker and audience—Asante even prefers the term *hearership* to *audience* because to him the former term suggests greater agency. Hearerships hold authority accountable.

Whatever the preferred term, the more that audience members are self-aware about their functioning and about the structural form of other discourses, the better. Participants who reflect critically on the overarching language structures in which they operate can make more informed choices or assessments concerning their involvement. What Asante calls a *rhetoric of structure* dictates foregone conclusions unless disrupted. "It does not matter," the argument goes, "if the language of the imperative is polite and gentle, so long as the imperative structure endures; a social environment has been created where one, for instance, gives orders, and the other is expected to obey" (p. 31). This reminds us of being called by our parents from some activity we thought pressing and asked to do chores or run errands. *Would you mop the kitchen floor for me? Do you want to go to the store for me?* We never misunderstood these utterances to be questions rather than commands. Obviously, it was not in our collective best interest to rebel. We would later have our chances. We are merely trying to drive home the point. If you comply completely with the terms of the discourse, you are stuck with the outcomes. Afrocentric rhetoric, given the salient feature of call-and-response and the enhanced role for hearers, provides a way, in political realms both small and large, to disidentify, as Asante terms it, from controlling structures. Recall the interaction of Willie Ricks and the audience in Greenwood mentioned in the last chapter.

Although the call-and-response dynamic is a hallmark, there is much more to the system of Afrocentric rhetoric. In fact, call-and-response is but one way to express *Nommo*, the intense African belief in the potency of the word. Smitherman (1977) explains in *Talkin and Testifyin*:

> All activities of men, and all movements in nature, rest on the word, on the productive power of the word, which is water and heat and seed and Nommo, that is, life force itself. . . . In traditional African culture, a newborn is a mere thing until his father gives and speaks his name. No medicine, potion, or magic of any sort is considered effective without accompanying words. So strong is the African belief in the power and absolute necessity of Nommo that all craftsmanship must be accompanied by speech.
>
> (p. 78)

Or as Toni Morrison remarked in a conversation with writer and critic Thomas LeClair, "It [the language] is the thing that black people love so much—the saying of words, holding them on the tongue, experimenting with them, playing with them. It's a love, a passion" (LeClair, 1981, p. 27).

Call-and-response is the communal invocation of "word-force" to establish harmony. As indicated, its polyphonic, improvisational, rhythmic nature accounts for the inventiveness, indeed the invention, of verbal styles from Black pulpit oratory to hip hop. Speaking of contemporary African-American preachers and rappers, Asante observes that they know what their African ancestors knew with their use of Nommo, that is, "that all magic is word magic" (1998, p. 60).

Nommo, then, infuses *orature*, which is defined as the "comprehensive body of oral discourse on every subject and in every genre of expression produced by a people" (p. 96). This is a more elaborate idea than *oratory*, which denotes the practice of eloquent public speaking. Orature includes vocality, drumming, storytelling, praise singing, naming, sermons, lectures, raps, the dozens, poetry, and humor (pp. 72, 96). Speakers in the tradition emphasize lyricism and style; they favor the poetic over strict lecturing. The goal is to fascinate as much as to instruct (p. 91). They employ prototypical tales, which in turn become *mythoforms* that produce variations to demonstrate the possibility of exerting control over social circumstances and prospects for a better future (pp. 108, 112). Myth and mythoforms are perhaps the most powerful resources that speakers in the tradition command, "the all-encompassing deep generator[s] of ideas and concepts in our living relations with our peers, friends, and ancestors" (p. 108). Principal myths, as Asante would label them, include Shine, Flying Africans, and Stagolee.

For example, consider the poet Etheridge Knight's rendition of the myth of Shine, a survivor of the ill-fated Titanic:

And, yeah, brother,
while white/America sings about the unsink
able molly brown
(who was hustling the titanic
when it went down)
I sing to thee of Shine
the stoker who was hip
enough to flee the fucking ship
and let the white folks drown
with screams on their lips
jumped his black ass into the dark sea, Shine did
broke free from the straining steel.
yeah, I sing of Shine
and how the millionaire banker stood on the deck
and pulled from his pocket a million dollar check
saying Shine Shine save poor me
and I'll give you all the money a black boy needs—
how Shine looked at the money and then at the sea
and said jump in muthafucka and swim like me—
and Shine swam on—Shine swam on—
how the banker's daughter ran naked on the deck
with her pinktits trembling and her pants round her neck
screaming Shine Shine save poor me
and I'll give you all the cunt a black boy needs—
how Shine said now cunt is good and that's no jive
but you got to swim not fuck to stay alive—
then Shine swam past a preacher afloat on a board
crying save me nigger Shine in the name of the Lord—
how the preacher grabbed Shine's arm and broke his stroke—
how Shine pulled his shank and cut the preacher's throat—
and Shine swam on—all alone.
And when news hit the shore that the titanic had sunk
Shine was up in Harlem damn near drunk—
and dancing in the streets.
yeah, damn near drunk and dancing in the streets.
                              (1968/2004, pp. 377–8)

As with all literature, the myth of Shine is open to several interpretations. It can be read as an instance of divine judgment on Jim Crow or as an expression of the ultimate superiority of black intelligence and self-reliance in the face of insensitive and foolish technocrats. Asante reads it as a story of self-discovery amid chaos (1998, p. 114). As he explains,

> In the moment of crisis, Shine recognizes that his condition was normally one of second-class status, although *he* could swim. This discovery gives him a power over the white and wealthy that he would never have achieved if it had not been for the sinking of the *Titanic*. The moral is not lost on the African American community: crisis has a way of equalizing everyone.
>
> (pp. 114–15)

The myth of Flying Africans likely originates from an Igbo rebellion on St. Simons Island in 1803. After being purchased in Savannah by agents representing John Couper and Thomas Spalding, the enslaved were put aboard ship for transport to St. Simons. During the trip they rebelled and chased the agents into the sea. Upon landing, the Igbo hid in the swamp and apparently died in Dunbar Creek. It is unclear, of course, how the historical tale of flight on land was transformed into a myth of aerial flight, but the story has endured in numerous variations. In the 1930s, when Wallace Quarterman was interviewed by members of the Federal Writers Project, he offered, "Ain't you heard about them? Well, at that time Mr. Blue he was the overseer and . . . Mr. Blue he go down one morning with a long whip for to whip them good. . . . Anyway, he whipped them good and they got together and stuck that hoe in the field and then . . . rose up in the sky and turned themselves into buzzards and flew right back to Africa. . . . Everybody knows about them" (Powell and Dobbs, 2017). Since Quarterman's time, there have been additional versions of the myth, including Virginia Hamilton's *The People Could Fly* (1985/2004) and Toni Morrison's *Song of Solomon* (1977).

Although Asante does not make the connection explicitly, he would perhaps consider Flying Africans stories to be expressions of what he calls the return myth (p. 162) or "one of the significant motifs of the African American experience" (p. 169). Speaking to its enduring relevance, he reasons, "If the African's initial reaction to bondage in a strange land was a persistent search for a way to return, decades of servitude and generations of discrimination have only reinforced the myth's power" (p. 169). Asante sees this myth as having been operative in the work of the leading Back-to-Africa political activists, Marcus Garvey and Bishop Henry McNeal Turner, and in the psychological embraces of African heritage.

The eve-of-the-millennium film *Belly* also illustrates the return myth. Trying to extract himself from a life of crime, Sincere (Nas) makes a suggestion to his wife Tionne (T-Boz):

> "Yo, T. T, I feel like it's time for us to, like, go up, go away from here. You know what I mean? I been thinking about it for a long time."
> "Where would we go?"

"T, let's go to Africa."

"Shit nigga please. Be for real.'"

"Yo, I never been more serious in my life. I mean, we been at the islands. We been everywhere. Who says we can't go to Africa?"

"I mean, but, I mean . . . I mean, I don't know. Africa's far."

"So what? I'm saying, just think about us. That's all we ever talk about. That's our dream. To go to our homeland. Where our roots are. Fuck it, man. You know what I'm sayin? Like, forget about money. Fuck everything. It's the chance of a lifetime. If me and you went, and the baby, yo. Just think. Maybe it's the right thing to do. Maybe not."

"Well, I'll think about it. I will think about it."

After a few more harrowing episodes of street life, including a home invasion and, in a separate incident, the wounding of Sincere, Tionne grows eager to depart. Sincere informs his friends and acquaintances about his upcoming journey, including his former crime partner, Tommy "Bundy" Brown (DMX), who is also apparently reconsidering his life's path and is a sympathetic listener:

"Yo, I'm going to Africa."

"Word?"

"Word."

"I'm a take some time out to reflect on the things that's happenin. You know, between you, me, the whole world."

"That's ill, Son. That's ill. What can I say but, you know, congratulations. Good luck on your trip to the Motherland."

Africa symbolizes the resolution of all problems. It is an unrealistic expectation, but the germane point is that the return myth is powerfully seductive, is deeply embedded in African-American culture, and has endured. At the end of the film, Sincere in a voiceover tells of his arrival in Africa, where "It felt right. It was harmony. It was like a whole new beginning."

Sincere's redirection is positive, but he does not reflect the rawest form of resistance in the Black psyche. That place is occupied by the Stagolee mythoform. Stagolee himself, according to Asante, "represents the radical impulse to challenge an authority that seeks to repress freedom, improvisation, and harmony" (p. 118). He is "an archetype of the rebel, the protest speaker, the revolutionary" (p. 122). Tough and uncensored, he is the leading badman of African-American culture. Rooted in the 1895 murder of Billy Lyons by hustler "Stag" Lee Shelton in St. Louis, Stagolee stories have proliferated in a wide array of forms. Here is one example:

And in walked the rollers [police];
They picked up Stag and carried him to court.
Judge told Stag, say, "Stag, I been wanting you for a long time."
Say, "I'm gon' give you twenty years."

Stag looked up at the Judge, say, "twenty years! Twenty years ain't no time.
I got a brother in Sing Sing doing one ninety-nine."

And then a ho walked in and to the courtroom's surprise
She pulled out two long forty-fives.
Stag grabbed one and shot his way to the courtroom do',
Tipping his hat to all the ladies once mo'.

(Dance, 2002b,"Stagolee," p. 490)

"Ultimately, Asante writes, "we seek to effect the great opposition in discourse
by calling upon this major mythoform" (1998, p. 122).

Yet the overall goal of Afrocentric rhetoric as a project beyond the Stagolee
mythoform is expansion not opposition. Its prevailing gesture is a humanistic
affirmation of cultures. It locates agency in the developers of African-American
discourse and contributes to a fuller account of rhetoric in general and to, as
indicated, an all-embracing humanistic vision.

A Tradition of Signifying

According to Google Scholar, Henry Louis Gates, Jr.'s *The Signifying Monkey: A
Theory of Afro-American Literary Criticism* (1988a) has been cited in text more
than 4,000 times, making it over the past thirty years perhaps the most popular
and relevant volume published about Black literature. But one should not be
fooled by the restrictiveness implied by the subtitle. Along with its immediate
predecessor, *Figures in Black: Words, Signs, and the "Racial Self"* (1987), the book
constitutes the central statement that Gates offers about rhetoric. Describing
his work, Gates confides, "my movement, then, is from hermeneutics to rhetoric
and semantics, only to return to hermeneutics once again" (1988a, p. 44). As
prelude to his brilliant explications of works in the Black literary tradition,
Gates theorizes what is "Black" in those texts aside from messages or the fact
of their production by what might be considered Black bodies, both unreliable
indicators to him of "Blackness." His book is thus an important rhetoric treatise
for at least four reasons: 1) it describes a system of figurations, 2) it is an argument about the composition elements required if literary texts are to evince
"Blackness, 3) it makes a case for how to write about the literature in question,
and 4) it is a self-conscious testament to African-American humanity and creativity. In short, Gates, armed with a rhetoric of African-American literature,
stands against the wholesale application of Euro-American critical theories to
Black texts and against the sole reliance on extra-literary matters.

Gates settles on the Signifying Monkey as the "figure-of-figures" (p. xxi).
This creature is related to Esu-Elegbara, who in Yoruba mythology is a trickster
and a messenger of the gods, and is one who is proficient at interpretation,
translation, and wordplay, including irony, indirection, double-entendre, and
satire. Counterparts or derivations of Esu-Elegbara are Legba in Benin, Exu
in Brazil, Papa Legba in Haiti, Echu-Elegua in Cuba, and Papa La Bas in the
United States. Gates surmises that the Signifying Monkey descends directly

from Cuban mythology because Echu-Elegua is often depicted with a monkey at his side (1987, p. 238).

Witness the African-American incarnation of Esu-Elegbara in action in one of numerous versions:

> The Monkey and the Lion got to talkin' one day.
> Monkey say, "There's a bad cat livin' down your way."
> He say, "You take this fellow to be your friend,
> But the way he talks about you is a sin;
> He say folks say you king, and that may be true,
> But he can whip the daylights outta you.
> And somethin' else I forgot to say:
> He talks about your mother in a hell of a way."
> Monkey say, "His name is Elephant, and he's not your friend."
> Lion say, "He don't need to be 'cause today will be his end."
> Say like a ball of fire and a streak of heat,
> The old Lion went rolling down the street.
> That Lion let out a terrible sneeze,
> And knocked the damn giraffe to his everlastin' knees.
> Now he saw Elephant sittin' under a tree,
> And he say, "Now you bring your big black butt to me."
> The Elephant looked at 'im out the corner of his eyes,
> And say, "Now little punk, go play with somebody your size."
> The Lion let out a roar and reared up six feet tall,
> Elephant just kicked him in the belly and laughed to see him fall.
> Now they fought all night and they fought all day;
> And I don't know how in hell that Lion ever got away.
> But the Lion was draggin' back through the jungle more dead than
>   alive,
> And that's when that Monkey start that signifying.
> He say, "Hey-y-y, Mr. Lion, you don't look so swell;
> Look to me like you caught a whole lotta hell!
> You call yourself a king and a ace,
> It's gon' take ninety yards o' sailcloth to patch yo' face.
> Now git on out from under my tree,
> Before I decide to drop my drawers and pee.
> Stop, don't let me hear you roar,
> or I'll come down outta this tree and beat your tail some more.
> Say the damn old Lion was sitting down there crying,
> And the Monkey just *kept* signifying.
> And then Monkey started jumpin' around
> And his foot slipped and he fell down.
> Like a ball of fire and a streak of heat,
> The old Lion was on him with all four feet.
> Say the Monkey looked up with tears in his eyes,
> And say, "Mr. Lion, I apologize!

Now, good buddy, in this jungle friends are few;
You know I was only playin' wit' you."
Monkey looked at Lion and saw he wasn't gon' get away,
So he decided to think of a bold damn play.
He say, "Mr. Lion, you ain't raisin' no hell,
Everybody in the jungle saw me when I fell.
Now if you let me up like a real man should,
I'll kick your butt all over these woods." The old Lion looked at 'im and
    jumped back for a hell of a fight
And in a split second the Monkey was damn near outta sight.
He jumped up in a tree higher than any human eye can see,
And say, "You dumb mammyjammer, don't you ever mess wid me!"
                                        ("The Signifying Monkey," pp. 492–4)

The monkey lacks the lion's physical power, but he definitely has something *for* a lion if necessary. He has elephants at his disposal. This trickster is a metaphor for how one grasps the totality of power dynamics in a given system and exerts a measure of control over circumstances despite operating at a physical or material disadvantage. It illustrates how the physically subordinate can get their meanings to matter by expertly using restricted codes in spaces where multiple codes operate. The lion remains disoriented, as well as in terrible shape, because in reading the monkey literally he cannot read him at all.

Gates posits that the Signifying Monkey is "the figure of a black rhetoric in the Afro-American speech community" and self-consciously embodies the speech characteristics of the Black vernacular (1988a, p. 53). Signifying is, therefore, in Black rhetoric, the "trope of tropes" (p. 51). To signify is to make meaning within a Black rhetorical world that exists alongside and in relation to a white one, a situation Gates describes as "parallel discursive universes" (p. 45). The same vocabulary items, *signify*, express fundamental opposition. For example, there is no way to indicate this difference with other terms. *Not sharp*, the opposite of *sharp*, can be communicated as *dull*. But one cannot label the opposite of *meaning* other than to say *not meaning*. Even *nonsense* and *meaningless* do not quite capture the distinction. The parallel words *signify* intriguingly look the same even as they index different rhetorical worlds. In the Black lexicon, *to signify* is to make meaning in Black.

This does not suggest the impossibility of translation, only a divide along a crucial linguistic marker that starkly epitomizes difference. Naturally, we can ascertain and discuss certain Black rhetorical production in relation to standard tropes, and Gates provides examples relative to the four master tropes so identified by Kenneth Burke (1941):

Your mama's a man	(metaphor)
Your daddy's one too	(irony)
They live in a tin can	(metonymy)
That smells like a zoo	(synecdoche) (In Gates, 1988a, p. 86)

But it is the ritual of Black signifying that calls these tropes, indeed all tropes, into being as Black subject matter.

The components of signification, according to Smitherman (1977), and then Gates (1988a), include the following traits:

1. indirect, circumlocution
2. metaphorical-imagistic (but images rooted in the everyday, real world)
3. humorous, ironic
4. rhythmic fluency and sound
5. teachy but not preachy
6. directed at person or persons usually present in the situational context
7. punning, play on words
8. introduction of the semantically or logically unexpected.

(Smitherman, p. 118; Gates, p. 94)

All of these features are on display in this passage from Chester Himes's novel, *Blind Man with a Pistol* (1969/1989), when those famous African-American police officers, Coffin Ed Johnson and Grave Digger Jones, explain a situation in Harlem to their white supervisor Anderson. Smitherman used the excerpt in *Talkin and Testifyin* and Gates in *The Signifying Monkey*:[2]

"I take it you've discovered who started the riot," Anderson said.
"We knew who it was all along," Grave Digger said.
"It's nothing we can do to him," Coffin Ed echoed.
"Why not, for God's sake?"
"He's dead," Coffin Ed said.
"Who?"
"Lincoln," Grave Digger said.
"He hadn't ought to freed us if he didn't want to make provisions to feed us," Coffin Ed said. "Anyone could have told him that."
"All right, all right, lots of us have wondered what he might have thought of the consequences," Anderson admitted. "But it's too late to charge him now."

Coffin Ed and Grave Digger continue to talk around, yet to, Anderson:

"Couldn't have convicted him anyway," Grave Digger said.
"All he'd have to do would be to plead good intentions," Coffin Ed elaborated. "Never was a white man convicted as long as he plead good intentions."
"All right, all right, who's the culprit this night here, in Harlem? Who's inciting these people to this senseless anarchy?"
"Skin," Grave Digger said.

(Himes, p. 135)

Smitherman, who obviously was a significant influence on Gates, as was anthropologist Claudia Mitchell-Kernan (1971), also analyzes the exchange relative to the eight characteristics listed above:

> Coffin Ed and Grave Digger show skillful use of indirection [1] to convey their message that rioting is caused by historical conditions of enslave-ment and white oppression. . . . The method of circumlocution [1] is used to teach Anderson but not in a sermonizing way. The siggin is directed at Anderson as a representative white liberal type in the Lincoln tradition, and thus it's being run on him to his face, not behind his back [6]. The two detectives are obviously introducing the unexpected [8], both in a logical and semantic sense. (Lincoln should have kept us enslaved if he wasn't going to make any provisions for us other than the many Harlems of the United States; thus eating as a slave is better than starving as a free man. Further, Anderson has asked a perfectly normal whodunit investigatory type question and instead gets a surprise sociological explanation [8].) There is rhythmic fluency [4] in the use of "freed us/feed us." The extended metaphor [2] of a mock trial is used to indict Lincoln and White America generally, as if to say they should be on trial and not the rioters. (Note courtroom terms like "charge him," "plead," and "convicted.") Further there is the metaphorical allusion [2] to the old saying, "The road to Hell is paved with good intentions." Finally, Grave Digger and Coffin Ed use metaphor, irony, and play on words [2, 3, 7] with their final *circumlocutory* response [1] that "skin" is responsible for the "senseless anarchy." By "skin" they are suggesting color, oppression, Lincoln, white liberal attitudes—in short, giving the same answer [5] they have been giving all along, in a different way and in one word. Like I said, they is baad!
>
> (1977, pp. 123–4)

Signifying also involves repetitions and reversals. In Black literary texts, for example, it reveals itself "as explicit theme, as implicit rhetorical strategy, and as a principle of literary history" (Gates, 1988a, p. 89). One illustration of the point is Gates's comparison of Richard Wright and Ralph Ellison:

> Ellison in his fictions Signifies upon Wright by parodying Wright's literary structures through repetition and difference. One can readily suggest the complexities of the parodying. The play of language, the Signifyin(g), starts with the titles. Wright's *Native Son* and *Black Boy*, titles connoting race, self, and presence, Ellison tropes with *Invisible Man*, with *invisibility* as an ironic response of absence to the would-be presence of blacks and natives, while *man* suggests a more mature and stronger status than either *son* or *boy*. Ellison Signifies upon Wright's distinctive version of naturalism with a complex rendering of modernism; Wright's re-acting protagonist, voiceless to the last, Ellison Signifies upon with a nameless protagonist. Ellison's character is nothing *but* voice, since it is he who shapes, edits, and

narrates his own tale, thereby combining action with the representation of action and defining reality by its representation. This unity of presence and representation is perhaps Ellison's most subtle reversal of Wright's theory of the novel as exemplified in *Native Son*. Bigger's voicelessness and powerlessness to act (as opposed to react) signify an absence, despite the metaphor presence found in the novel's title; the reverse obtains in *Invisible Man*, where the absence implied by invisibility is undermined by the presence of the narrator as the author of his own text.

(p. 106)

Of course, we can lengthen the chain of signification. Himes, for example, in his 1945 novel *If He Hollers Let Him Go*, reverses Bigger Thomas before Ellison does by creating the character Bob Jones. In fact, Jones, the first-person narrator, discusses Bigger explicitly:

> "I think Richard Wright is naïve," Polly said.
> "Aren't we all?" I said.
> "*Native Son* turned my stomach," Arline said. "It just proved what the white Southerner has always said about us; that our men are rapists and murderers."
> "Well, I will agree that the selection of Bigger Thomas to prove the point of Negro oppression was an unfortunate choice," Leighton said.
> "What do you think, Mr. Jones?" Cleo asked.
> I said, "Well, you couldn't pick a better person than Bigger Thomas to prove the point. But after you prove it, then what? Most white people I know are quite proud of having made Negroes into Bigger Thomases."
> (1945/2002, p. 88)

Moreover, *Native Son*'s influence on Lorraine Hansberry's (1959) play, *A Raisin in the Sun*, is unmistakable. The Youngers, like the Thomases, live on the south side of Chicago. Walter Lee Younger, like Bigger, works as a chauffeur. The difference in age between Bigger (20) and Walter Lee (35) is virtually the same as the time span between the publication of Wright's novel (1940) and the setting (1956) of Hansberry's play. So Bigger would be Walter Lee's age had he lived. Both the novel and the play open early in the morning. The first sounds in both are the ringing of an alarm clock and the urgent voice of a domineering woman. The similarities don't end there, but the point is made. Hansberry avoids the tragic ending and focuses on family triumph, on thriving in an environment instead of succumbing to it.

We see echoes of Bigger in present-day cultural productions such as the television series *Power*. Shawn is a chauffeur—dresses almost exclusively in the one chauffeur's suit given to him—and shares Bigger's penchant for abysmal decision-making. He pursues a romantic relationship with the wife of his boss and pledges allegiance to his own corrupt father. Not quite as ineloquent as Bigger, he nonetheless never speaks effectively back to authority, particularly

the authority of his father, who, ironically, betrays him and becomes his execu-
tioner (Jackson, Macedon, and McKay, 2015).

Gates's discussion of the African-American literary tradition is compelling
overall but gives rhetoricians concerned with more than formalism a few dis-
concerting pauses. He asserts, "a poem above all is atemporal" (1987, p. 33). But
in fact poems are multi-temporal; their meanings are not fixed but are, rather,
open across generations. Peculiarly, he claims for a poem—static, transhistorical
status—what he would not claim for any subject who writes a poem. Furthermore, he opines that poetry does not preach well (p. 32) and that "the black
poet is far more than a mere point of consciousness of the community . . . he or
she is the point of consciousness of the language" (p. 178). However, poetry as
a genre is perfectly suited to conveying preachments, exhortation, or instruction, though individual poets may or may not excel in this regard. And it is the
case that some people do not like or privilege poetry that preaches, but that is
a different matter. The relationship of the poet to community consciousness is
often stronger than signaled by the adjective *mere*. It is preferable to view the
poet both as the point of consciousness of the community *and* as the point of
consciousness of the language.

Similarly, when Gates endorses the premise of professors at a Yale conference
that "Afro-American literature is above all an act of language" (Gates, 1987,
p. 44), we respond that it is, rather, an act of language *along with* everything else
it is, including being social and political commentary.[3] The writers that Gates
theorizes about respond not only to language as language but to political positions and to arguments about identity and representation. Having conceded
the social basis of Black rhetoric, one cannot logically reduce Black rhetoric to
a linguistic game apart from social and political grounding. Gates's proclama-
tions are certainly understandable given the critical practices he counters, that
is, the reduction of Black texts to message vehicles or social sciences studies
with little or no attention to technical achievements or even structural genius.
But he may have gone overboard in reaction, perhaps partly because he wanted
to throw shade on politics left of his own liberalism. However, there is no deny-
ing his impressive interpretive contributions or his major role in conceptual-
izing and promoting the study of African-American rhetoric.

Rhetorics of Black Feminism

Spirited semantic work accompanies discussions of Black feminism. The concept refers generally to identity formation and initiatives for social change
fueled by the experiences and perspectives of Black women. Naturally, within
this paradigm exists a cluster of ideologies. So while in our view Black feminism remains a useful and convenient descriptor, it does not, as we shall see,
precisely label the thinking of everyone we would include in the framework.

The term *Black feminism* dates back to the 1960s. Feelings of exclusion
formed in response to the sexism inside Black political movements and the
racism inside white feminist groups motivated some African-American women

to create their own alliances such as the National Black Feminist Organization (NBFO), founded in New York City in 1973 by the likes of Doris Wright, Flo Kennedy, Faith Ringgold, and Michele Wallace. Regarding her experience at an early meeting of the NBFO, Alice Walker wrote in 1974,

> We sat together and talked and knew no one would think, or say, 'Your thoughts are dangerous to black unity and a threat to black men.' Instead, all the women understood that we gathered together to assure understanding among black women, and that understanding among women is not a threat to anyone who intends to treat women fairly.
>
> (1974/1984, p. 273)

However, some NBFO delegates sought a more radical economic agenda than was deducible from the dominant tone in the organization, which was moderate. Moreover, these delegates wanted to shine a spotlight on the specific issues confronting Black lesbians. As a result, Barbara Smith, Demita Frazier, and others established the Combahee River Collective in Boston in 1974 to clarify further their politics and activism. As the group stipulated in their most famous document, "A Black Feminist Statement," composed in 1978,

> The most general statement of our politics at the present time would be that we are actively committed to struggling against racial, sexual, heterosexual, and class oppression and see as our particular task the development of integrated analysis and practice based upon the fact that the major systems of oppression are interlocking. The synthesis of these oppressions creates the conditions of our lives. As black women we see black feminism as the logical political movement to combat the manifold and simultaneous oppressions that all women of color face.
>
> (1978/2009, p. 3)

As the 1970s extended into the hip-hop era and the hip-hop era extended into the 1980s and beyond, cultural critics such as Joan Morgan (1999) and Aisha Durham (2007) added *hip-hop feminism* to the common lexicon to announce the presence of those who are inclined toward feminism and also view hip-hop culture as essential to their sense of themselves and to how they function. Author of *When Chickenheads Come Home to Roost. . . . My Life as a Hip-Hop Feminist*," Morgan recounts her acceptance of the term *feminist* during a contentious discussion with three men:

> *It's simple. I love black men like I love no other. And I'm not talking sex or aesthetics, I'm talking about loving y'all enough to be down for the drama— stomping anything that threatens your existence. Now only a fool loves that hard without asking for the same in return. So yeah, I demand that black men fight sexism with the same passion they battle racism. I want you to annihilate anything that endangers sista's welfare—including violence against women—because my*

> survival walks hand in hand with yours. So, my brotha, if loving y'all fiercely
> and wanting it back makes me a feminist then I'm a feminist. So be it.
>
> (pp. 44–5)

Durham, for her part, defines hip-hop feminism as

> a socio-cultural, intellectual and political movement grounded in the situ-
> ated knowledge of women of color from the post-Civil Rights generation
> who recognize culture as a pivotal site for political intervention to chal-
> lenge, resist, and mobilize collectives to dismantle systems of exploitation.
>
> (pp. 304–5)

Over the years, some thinkers have preferred to dispense with the marker
feminism altogether. Walker, for example, coined the now-popular term *womanism*, which is synonymous with *Black feminism* but suggests different cultural
shading. The locution derives, Walker explains,

> from the black folk expression of mothers to female children, 'You acting
> womanish,' i.e., like a woman. Usually referring to outrageous, audacious,
> courageous or *willful* behavior. Wanting to know more and in greater depth
> than is considered 'good' for one. Interested in grown-up doings. Act-
> ing grown up. Being grown up. Interchangeable with another black folk
> expression: 'You trying to be grown.' Responsible. In charge. *Serious*.
>
> (1984, p. xi)

Clenora Hudson-Weems (1994) ranges a bit farther semantically in coin-
ing the term *Africana womanism*. Walker does not reject *Black feminism* in
her definition; Hudson-Weems does, judging that the word *feminist* essentially
means the concerns of white women. Moreover, she intends the label *Africana*
to convey a strong link to African culture and thus explicitly align her conception with Afrocentrism.

Other neologisms are sure to follow. But above or perhaps despite the issues
of definition, four grounding tropes seem to exist in what we consider Black-
feminist rhetoric:

1. the self-conscious verbal assertion of requisite Black female presence
2. commentary about the exercise of a Black female voice speaking against
    male domination
3. the ironic assertion of high-achieving Black womanhood, and
4. the positing of triple exploitation.

The first two tropes are exemplified in Anna Julia Cooper's remarkable 1892
text *A Voice from the South*. Reflecting on Martin Delaney, the estimable African-
American activist who died seven years prior, Cooper recalled that when
Delany, a "race man," appeared at special state functions, he would proclaim

that the Black race attended with him. Cooper, however, reasoned that a man could not authentically represent African Americans on the whole. Therefore, she articulated one of her signature dictums: "Only the Black WOMAN can say '*when and where I enter, in the quiet, undisputed dignity of my womanhood, without violence and without suing or special patronage, then and there the whole Negro race enters with me*'" (1892/1988, p. 31, emphasis original). The understanding is that no social or political project could adequately express African-American aspirations unless the full presence of African-American women was central. One could argue that Cooper erred in reading Delany's metaphorical expression literally. Furthermore, "quiet" might not be the most effective pitch to make today to many feminist or pro-feminist audiences. Nonetheless, Cooper hit the mark with her conclusion. Her comment was actually not so much about Delany; he was but provocation. She correctly spoke to the great gender imbalance among established African-American leadership. In any case, her pronouncement has resonated ever since and is a powerful composing tool for speakers and writers. This is signaled most markedly by the title and epigraph of Paula Giddings's 1984 *When and Where I Enter: The Impact of Black Women on Race and Sex in America*.

Giddings's book also contains examples of what we may now call the when-and-where-I-enter trope, some of which predate Cooper's memorable phrasing. Giddings points out, for example, that, in 1849, Black women threatened to boycott a Black convention in Ohio if not given a prominent role. Six years later, at a Black convention in Philadelphia, Mary Ann Shadd Cary gained admission after she protested vigorously (p. 59). In both cases, Black women deemed the political gathering illegitimate if it lacked their significant involvement. The National Association of Colored Women (NACW), founded in 1896, represents another self-conscious expression of "entry." Josephine St. Pierre Ruffin explained at a national convention in Boston that led to the establishment of the NACW, "We are not alienating or withdrawing. We are only coming to the front" (Giddings, 1984, p. 95).[4] She announced the group's self-determining participation, including of course their physical presence, in the public sphere.

Closely connected to physical presence is vocal display. One not only must show up, one must show out. As Cooper assessed the matter, "'tis women's strongest vindication for speaking that *the world needs to hear her voice*. It would be subversive of every human interest if the cry of one-half the human family be stifled" (p. 121, emphasis original). Without using the term *rhetoric*, Cooper nonetheless made the case for rhetorical culture, the consideration and negotiation of provisional truths by individuals and groups in free-flowing civil exchange. Such conduct was, in her view, the essence of democracy. She adduced,

> No one belief can be supreme in America. All interests must be consulted, all claims conciliated. Exchange among many putting forth their argumentative best is the best defense against tyranny. Compromise and

concession, liberality and toleration were the conditions of the nation's founding and are the *sine qua non* of its continued existence.

(pp. 164–5)

Cooper pointed out that even oligarchs have to pretend that service and not supremacy is their aim, which is certainly an instance, though unfortunately not an unfamiliar one, of rhetoric being used in bad faith (pp. 165–8).

Perhaps the classic comment on the role of a Black female voice belongs to Zora Neale Hurston. In her 1937 novel, *Their Eyes Were Watching God*, Janie's voyage to "voice" is one of the central dynamics. Her second husband, Joe Starks, had always desired to be a "big voice," but he harbors no desire to see his wife become one as well (1937/1978, p. 48). He severely limits her opportunities to speak in public. He does not let her address crowds and keeps her from kibitzing with some of the town's great raconteurs, who gather on the porch of his store. For her years of acquiescence, Janie is maintained in material comfort. She is no match for her husband in verbal jousting anyway until she spends years learning to decipher him (p. 120). As she approaches forty, she no longer holds him in awe and deposes him with words, the showdown occurring when he attempts to embarrass her in front of customers simply because she improperly cut some chewing tobacco. However, unlike in the past, she startles him with her aggressiveness and skill:

> "I god amighty! A woman stay round uh store till she get old as Methu-salem and still can't cut a little thing like a plug of tobacco! Don't stand dere rollin' yo' pop eyes at me wid yo' rump hangin' nearly to yo' knees!"
>
> A big laugh started off in the store but people got to thinking and stopped. It was funny if you looked at it right quick, but it got pitiful if you thought about it awhile. It was like somebody snatched off part of a woman's clothes while she wasn't looking and the streets were crowded. Then too, Janie took the middle of the floor to talk right into Jody's face, and that was something that hadn't been done before.
>
> "Stop mixin' up mah doings wid mah looks, Jody. When you git through tellin' me how tuh cut uh plug uh tobacco, then you kin tell me whether mah behind is on straight or not."
>
> "Wha—whut's dat you say, Janie? You must be out yo' head."
>
> "Naw, Ah ain't outa mah head neither."
>
> "You must be. Talkin' any such language as dat."
>
> "You de one started talkin' under people's clothes. Not me."
>
> "Whut's the matter wid you, nohow? You ain't no young girl to be get-tin' insulted 'bout yo' looks. You ain't no young courtin' gal. You'se uh ole woman, nearly forty."

(pp. 121–2)

Caught off guard, Joe is ill equipped to handle his wife on this occasion. They exchange a few barbs about each other's age and general appearance before Janie delivers the *coup de grace*:

You big-bellies round here and put on a lot of brag, but 'tain't nothin' to it but yo' big voice. Humph! Talkin' 'bout *me* lookin old! When you pull down yo' britches, you look lak de change uh life.

(p. 123)

The stunned audience immediately grasps the import of Janie's assault:

"Great God from Zion!" Sam Watson gasped. "Y'all really playin' de dozens tuhnight."

"Wha—whut's dat you said?" Joe challenged, hoping his ears had fooled him.

"You heard her, you ain't blind," Walter taunted.

"Ah ruther be shot with tacks than tuh hear dat 'bout mahself," Lige Moss commiserated.

(p. 123)

Joe stands before the town humiliated, a pitiable figure in a place where he has long been a dominant figure. Having lost control over his own tongue and over Janie's, he strikes her. Eventually, he moves out of the bedroom and more or less ignores his wife, though he is still reeling from her surprising offensive. A decline in health mirrors his rhetorical fall, and he soon expires. Janie with her now-strong voice is on the path to a much more empowered life.

The ironic assertion of high-achieving Black womanhood was most succinctly expressed by Sojourner Truth. At an 1851 woman's rights convention in Akron, the secretary, Marius Robinson, captured part of her performance:

I want to say a few words about this matter. I am a woman's rights [*sic*]. I have as much muscle as any man, and can do as much work as any man. I have plowed and reaped and husked and chopped and mowed, and can any man do more than that? I have heard much about sexes being equal; I can carry as much as any man, and can eat as much too, if I can get it. I am as strong as any man that is now.

(Foner and Branham, 1998, p. 228)

Another account, written years later by Frances Dana Gage, who presided over the conference, added the phrase "arn't I a woman?":

That man over there says that women need to be helped into carriages, and lifted over ditches, and to have the best place everywhere. Nobody ever helps me into carriages, or over mud puddles, or gives me any best place! And arn't I a woman? Look at me! Look at my arm! I have plowed, and planted, and gathered into barns, and no man could head me! And arn't I a woman? I could work as much and eat as much as a man—when I could get it—and bear the lash as well! And arn't I a woman? I have borne thirteen children, and seen them most all sold off into slavery, and when I cried out with a mother's grief, none but Jesus heard me! And arn't I a woman?

(Foner and Branham, 1998, pp. 227–8)

Neither account is a literal transcript, but the second account is of added interest to rhetoric scholars because of the refrain. Sojourner's question, assuming she posed it, is not a genuine interrogative.[5] The brilliant rhetorical question is actually the insistence on recognition of the fact that she was, indeed, marvelously and irrefutably a woman. She linked the shortest statement of subjectivity in the English language—I—with limitless Black female possibility. She ironically succeeded as a "man"—in the field and on the platform—to make a case for women. Her words, like Cooper's, are reflected in the title of a Black-feminist volume, in this case, bell hooks' *Ain't I a Woman?"* published in 1981. Truth's words have even crossed over onto the cover of a historical study, Deborah Gray White's 1987 *Ar'n't I a Woman?: Female Slave in the Plantation South*, as well as Ilona Linthwaite's multicultural poetry anthology, the 1988 *Ain't I a Woman: A Book of Poetry from around the World*.

Walker noted how she was pleased when she realized that Sojourner Truth was also her name, meaning that *Sojourner* equals *Walker* and *Alice* is a word for truth in Old Greek (1989, pp. 97–8). Not surprisingly, Walker presents in fiction a character strikingly similar to Sojourner Truth. Early in the short story "Everyday Use" (1973), the first-person narrator, Mrs. Johnson, thinks wishfully about being a petite, witty woman who appears on television with Dee, who is the elder of her two daughters, the one better educated and more glamorous. However, Mrs. Johnson abruptly shifts to an accurate self-description:

In real life I am a large, big-boned woman with rough, man-working hands. In the winter I wear flannel nightgowns to bed and overalls during the day. I can kill and clean a hog as mercilessly as any man. My fat keeps me hot in zero weather. I can work outside all day, breaking ice to get water for washing; I can eat pork liver cooked over the open fire minutes after it comes steaming from the hog. One winter I knocked a bull calf straight in the brain between the eyes with a sledge hammer and had the meat hung up to chill before nightfall.

(p. 48)

The double irony in her statement is that although she would acknowledge "I was always better at a man's job" (p. 50), she is a remarkable woman in the same mold as Sojourner Truth and, despite possessing only a second-grade education, she is a wiser mother than any version of herself about which she dreamed. When Dee, now a worldly cultural nationalist who had changed her name to Wangero, visits her and Maggie at their home in rural Georgia, Dee seeks to collect artifacts that are symbols of her heritage. Her intended haul includes two quilts made largely from some of her grandmother's dresses. But Mrs. Johnson had been saving the quilts to give to Maggie as a wedding present.

As Dee grows more insistent, Maggie, accustomed to losing to Dee in nearly every way, concedes the latest prize: "She can have them. . . . I can 'member Grandma Dee without the quilts" (p. 58).

Mrs. Johnson rejects Maggie's proposition:

> I looked at her hard. She had filled her bottom lip with checkerberry snuff and it gave her face a kind of hangdog look. It was Grandma Dee and Big Dee [her aunt] who taught her how to quilt herself. She stood there with her scarred hands hidden in the folds of her skirt. She looked at her sister with something like fear but she wasn't mad at her. This was Maggie's portion. This was the way she knew God to work.
> When I looked at her like that something hit me in the top of my head and ran down to the soles of my feet. Just like when I'm in church and the spirit of God touches me and I get happy and shout. I did something I never had done before: hugged Maggie to me, then dragged her on into the room, snatched the quilts out of Miss Wangero's hands and dumped them into Maggie's lap. Maggie just sat there on my bed with her mouth open.
> (p. 58)

Mrs. Johnson had once saved Maggie from a fire, one that had scarred her daughter. Inspired by religious revelation in the same manner as Sojourner Truth, she again protects Maggie and affirms her at a critical psychological moment.

The popularization of the construct of triple exploitation, also called triple jeopardy or triple oppression, is traceable to two Black female radicals: Louise Thompson Patterson and Claudia Jones. As a delegate to the founding convention of the National Negro Congress in February 1936, Patterson attended a session on Black women and labor. A resolution to unionize domestic workers, promote housewives' leagues, and organize women's groups into a united front was offered and adopted. In the preamble, the proposers noted that Black women were subjected to "three-fold exploitation as women, as workers, and as Negroes." Reflecting on the conference for the magazine *The Woman Today*, Patterson (1936), writing then as Louise Thompson, penned, "Over the whole land, Negro women meet this triple exploitation—as workers, as women, and as Negroes. About 85 per cent of all Negro women workers are domestics, two-thirds of the two million domestic workers in the United States" (p. 14). She theoretically linked the plight of Black Southern domestic workers and field hands to the circumstances of the Black women who gathered daily in Bronx Park to be chosen for day labor at 10 or 15 cents per hour, a practice, known as the Bronx Slave Market, that recently had been exposed in the *Crisis* by Ella Baker and Marvel Cooke (1935).

If Louise Thompson Patterson was, as Du Bois declared in 1934, "the leading colored woman in the Communist movement in this country" (p. 327), Jones, perpetually hounded by government authorities, precariously assumed that mantle in the 1940s. In 1949, she published an influential essay in *Political*

Affairs titled "An End to the Neglect of the Problems of the Negro Woman!" Employing a variation of the when-and-where-I-enter trope, Jones wrote,

> The bourgeoisie is fearful of the militancy of the Negro woman, and for good reason. The capitalists know, far better than many progressives seem to know, that once Negro women undertake action, the militancy of the whole Negro people, and thus of the anti-imperialist coalition, is greatly enhanced.
>
> (p. 3)

Then, turning to the idea of triple exploitation, Jones proceeded to argue, "Negro women—as workers, as negroes, and as women—are the most oppressed stratum of the whole population" (p. 4). During her far-reaching discussion of labor-market discrimination, white-chauvinist stereotypes, and justice-system racism, Jones reiterated, regarding Black women, "the special oppression she faces as Negro, as woman, and as worker" (p. 6). Following the lead of Patterson and Jones, the concept of triple exploitation has become a staple of Black-feminist discourse, indeed of all discourse that has as its aim a serious discussion of the political situation of African-American women.

Scholars continue to deepen our tropological understanding. One note-worthy example is Gwendolyn Pough's discussion of *wreck*. Contemplating "Black womanist traditions and a Hip-Hop present," (p. 13), Pough (2004) is concerned with the

> ways the rhetorical practices of Black women participants in Hip-Hop culture bring wreck—that is, moments when Black women's discourses disrupt dominant masculine discourses, break into the public sphere, and in some way impact or influence the U.S. imaginary, even if that influence is fleeting.
>
> (p. 76)

She cites, among others, Queen Latifah (1993) and Eve (1999) as exemplars who have brought wreck (Pough, p. 101). Pough describes a *rhetoric of wreck* (pp. 75–92), a hip-hop extension of speech acts associated with Black women, such as *talking back*, a voiced resistance against the marginalization of Black women (p. 80); *going off*, an expression of rage, a controlled expression, in Pough's formulation, for speaking back to power to effect change (pp. 80–1); *turning it out*, a verbal strategy that when fused with *bringing wreck* is a carefully constructed response to stereotypes and disrespect regarding Black women (p. 81); having a niggerbitch fit, a public and strategic expression of indignation, best done collectively (pp. 81–2); and *being a diva*, being a hip-hop version of someone committed to the uplift of herself and others (pp. 82–3). Although not always in the service of expressly feminist politics, *wreck* is an insightful way to frame various interventions inside an overall Black-feminist rhetorical project.

Other recent contributions are also worth mentioning. The Crunk Feminist Collective (Cooper, Morris, and Boylorn, 2017) offers a trio of incisive terms. *Hip hop generation feminism* is

> our riff on the term 'hip hop feminism' coined by Joan Morgan in 1999. We add the term 'generation' to reflect the fact that we grew up as members of the hip hop generation and are shaped by the terms of this historical and cultural moment. Unlike hip hop feminism, hip hop generation feminism does not demand any particular allegiance to hip hop culture beyond acknowledging how the moment has shaped our politics and worldview.
>
> (p. 326)

Crunk feminism denotes "our brand of hip hop (generation) feminism, which centers the high-energy and percussive nature of crunk music[6] together with a clear commitment to dismantling patriarchy" (pp. 325–6). *Ratchet feminism* was coined by CFC member Britney Cooper to refer to "critiques of sexism and patriarchy that happen in otherwise 'ratchet' spaces.[7] Also refers to unlikely female friendships forged in the midst of complicated romantic relationship situations (e. g., between a man's girlfriend and his 'baby mama'" (p. 328).

Moya Bailey (2010) proposes the term *misogynoir*, a portmanteau combining the English word *misogyny* with the French word for *black*, that is, *noir*, to describe acts of contempt or prejudice directed specifically at Black women. The word entered the mainstream in August 2016 when singer Katy Perry incorporated it into an expression of support on Twitter for actress/comedian Leslie Jones, who had become the victim of racist and sexist cyber attacks. Bailey did not view Perry's usage as a negative development, but she did have reservations:

> We see allies getting a lot of points for using terminology that marginalized communities have been using for a while, like when men talk about feminism or white people talk about racism. . . . There's a real celebration of those instances as opposed to a willingness to listen to the people most affected.
>
> (Solis, 2016)

Yet, Bailey's coinage seems destined to remain a valuable item in an ever-expanding Black-feminist rhetorical toolbox. As she suggests,

> I think we have to refine language in a lot of different ways so we can actually come up with solutions that help the communities we want to address. . . . When you use language that's generic or unspecific you can get at some of the problem, but not all of it.
>
> (Solis, 2016)

Notes

1. Linguist Geneva Smitherman considers call-and-response, or call-response, to be one of the four Black Modes of Discourse, along with signification, tonal semantics, and narrative sequencing (1977, pp. 101–66).
2. *Talkin and Testifyin*, pp. 122–3; *Signifying Monkey*, pp. 96–7.
3. This refers to the two-week seminar, "Afro-American Literature: From Critical Approach to Course Design," funded by the National Endowment for the Humanities and directed by Robert B. Stepto. The statement that Gates quotes appears in the follow-up volume, *Afro-American Literature: The Reconstruction of Instruction* (Fisher and Stepto, 1979, p. 234).
4. At the convention in Boston, delegates founded the National Federation of Afro-American Women and chose Margaret Murray Washington to be president. The following year, at a meeting in Washington, DC, the Federation merged with the National League of Colored Women, headed by Mary Church Terrell, to form the National Association of Colored Women. Terrell was chosen to be president.
5. Philip S. Foner and Robert James Branham addressed the controversy about the various accounts of the speech: "The four extant contemporary transcriptions of Truth's speech differ substantially from Gage's text; none of the four, most notably, includes the famous phrase 'Ar'n't I a Woman?' (changed to 'A'n't' by [Elizabeth Cady] Stanton) by which the speech has come to be known, although all contain similar sentiments, and Truth may have used the phrase in reference to the familiar abolitionist slogan, 'Am I not a woman and a sister?'" (1998, p. 227).
6. Brittney Cooper, Susana Morris, and Robin Boylorn (2017) define crunk: "A Southern hip hop term originally used beginning in the 1990s by Lil Jon and the East Side Boyz. Refers to excitability, hyperness, and high energy. Some argue that the word is a mash-up of 'crazy' and 'drunk.' It also refers to the high energy of cranking something up" (p. 325).
7. Brittney Cooper, Susana Morris, and Robin Boylorn (2017) define ratchet(ness): "Refers to a Southern working-class mode of both play and resistance that is unconcerned with social propriety, often engages in profane social behaviors (like overtly sexual dancing or unapologetic use of profanity), and adamantly refuses the aspiration to be respectable. The term in its current iteration was first used by Anthony Mandigo of Shreveport, Louisiana, in a 1999 song called "Do da Ratchet," but has in the ensuing years been taken up as a class-inflected slang term characterizing behaviors that lack respectability or decorum" (p. 327).

5   Technology and African-American Rhetoric

In the allegorical novel *Invisible Man* (1952/1995), the unnamed narrator takes a job at Liberty Paints, where the best-selling product is Optic White, a brilliant shade of paint that is produced by stirring several drops of a black fluid into every can. Workers perform this task as the product is prepped for shipment. However, the key to the overall production of Optic White is the engineering skill of an elderly African-American, Lucius Brockway, a self-taught practitioner who expertly cooks raw materials in high-pressure tanks in the basement of one of the plant's buildings. He is the indispensable "*machine inside the machine*" (p. 217). The narrator is tasked with assisting him, which includes the crucial task of monitoring the pressure gauges on the tanks. During an altercation between the narrator and Brockway, which erupted because the hidebound Brockway suspects the narrator of associating with unionists and threatens his life, they ignore the gauges. At least one of the tanks explodes, and the narrator is badly injured. After a stay in the factory hospital, where he is subjected to shock therapy and cannot recall his identity, the narrator eventually is released.

In these episodes, the author Ralph Ellison artfully speaks to the fact that African-American experiences have always been technologized. After all, 100 million New World Africans did not *swim* across the Atlantic Ocean. And the most dramatic increase in the slave population in the United States was spurred by the invention of the cotton gin.[1] It is not surprising, then, that Ellison explores the idea that White supremacy is fundamentally related to technological control. Moreover, questioning and sometimes contesting technological control is essential to the evolution of Black consciousness, though the journey is never easy, as the narrator knows:

> I fell to plotting ways of short-circuiting the machine. Perhaps if I shifted my body about so that the two nodes would come together—No, not only was there no room but it might electrocute me. I shuddered. Whoever else I was, I was no Samson. I had no desire to destroy myself even if it destroyed the machine; I wanted freedom, not destruction. It was exhausting, for no matter what scheme I conceived, there was one constant flaw—myself. There was no getting around it. I could no more escape than I could think

of my identity. Perhaps, I thought, the two things are involved with each other. When I discover who I am, I'll be free.

(p. 243)

Whereas Brockway is locked into an identity—he is complicit with the system—the narrator continues on a quest for freedom. At the end of his tale, he is contemplating his life while living in yet another basement, a secret abode in a building that rents only to Whites. He draws electricity into his well-lit den by tapping a power line owned by Monopolated Light & Power. He claims to wage battle with the company because it allows him to feel his "vital aliveness" (p. 7). He is a forerunner to hip-hoppers in New York City who did the same thing to Consolidated Edison in the 1970s for the same reason, tapped into power lines to connect DJ equipment in the parks and streets of a post-civil-rights urban landscape and come *alive*. The narrator, also a precursor to the pump-up-the-volume, multi-turntable exploits of DJs, plans to acquire four radio-phonographs to add to the one that he currently possesses. Wishing to feel the vibration of music with his whole body, he plans to play simultaneously five recordings of Louis Armstrong performing "What Did I Do to Be so Black and Blue?" (pp. 7–8).

Thus, following Ellison as well as Armstrong, to conceive of African-American rhetoric in relation to technology becomes one more way of exploring the blue note of Black experience in this society. A central query is whether engagement with technologies inside this society is worth it. It is a remixing of the old question of whether there is reason to believe that the grand experiment of American democracy can ever truly work. Black engagements with technologies and technology issues show in yet another way that African-American rhetoric reflects the struggles of living an existence that consistently vacillates between American Dream and American Nightmare, with some elements of both being always present.

Indeed, African-American tropes of struggle, separatism, escape, flight, Decline of the West, and pluralistic possibility all find expression in constructs of technology. For instance, consider the mothership motif. In the 1930s, Wallace Fard Muhammad, a founder of the Nation of Islam, taught that a Mother Plane, a wheel-shaped spaceship, would facilitate Armageddon. It would be built in Japan, and its technology would be integrated into 1,500 smaller spaceships, which would be armed with bombs and piloted by Black scientists in the effort to drown racist America in a lake of fire (Clegg, pp. 64–7). At one time or another, this line of reasoning was a staple of public lectures by Elijah Muhammad, Malcolm X, and Louis Farrakhan.[2] Although quite fanciful, the idea often registered as no more far-fetched to recruits than did most prophecies. Rather, the notion of the Mother Plane had rhetorical force precisely because it drew from biblical prophecy, at that time still the most valued preachment for African Americans. The shape of the Mother Plane was derived from the description of wheels in Ezekiel 10: 2–11. The mission stems partly from Revelation 19:20.

The teaching also gained traction because of its overtures to nationalism and technology. Many African Americans felt that the Japanese were the champions of people of color, a belief that persisted widely until World War II.[3] It was an important part of the storyline that the Mother Plane be built in Japan, especially given the military strength that Japan projected as evidenced by its development of advanced weaponry, in particular the *Yamato* class of battleships. Wallace Fard Muhammad was likely also influenced (Clegg, pp. 43–4) by the wave of science fiction movies about Mars, including *A Trip to Mars* (Méliès, 1903), *England Invaded* (Stormont, 1909), *A Message from Mars* (Karger, 1921), and *Mars Calling* (Neill,1923). Aerospace technology was new, and Americans were fascinated by the prospects of interplanetary travel and life beyond Earth. The tale of the Mother Plane, whether intended to be literal or metaphorical, made it clear that White hegemony did not exist either in the cosmos or in eternity.

The mothership of popular culture, namely, the pronouncements, lyrics, and iconic stage prop of Parliament-Funkadelic, seems to have been a secular and spectacular spinoff. The mothership is the home of P-Funk; it is a space of heightened creativity and freedom for citizens of the universe. The actual stage prop was constructed after the release of the 1975 album *Mothership Connection* and first landed at a concert in Houston in 1976. In its fantasy, the mothership is real. In fact, a replica is docked in the Smithsonian National Museum of African American History and Culture. It also, in continuing the tradition, lent its name to a short-story collection (Campbell and Austin, *Mothership*, 2013).

Part of what is at stake in highlighting African-American engagements with technologies is the imperative to disrupt positivistic assumptions that technologies are value free or value neutral. As historian Bruce Sinclair (2004) asserted,

> We can give meaning and form to our technologies as consumers, and we can shape their applications through politics, but it is important to understand that they do not come to us as a given. They are not the result of a neutral process, and they are certainly not the consequence of some inevitable technical logic. They are the result of choices, of social processes, and consequently they embody interests, positions, and attitudes.
>
> (pp. 11–12)

Disabusing ourselves of this fallacy of technological neutrality helps us to understand, as Ellison knew, that technological systems are implicated in enduring systems of exclusion and oppression as well as being sites of Black agency, techne, knowledge, and creativity. In short, we must range beyond instrumentalist views of technologies, beyond the idea that what matters with technology is only the device, the social-networking site, or the code that lies just beneath any digital interface. Technologies are interconnected systems of tools, politics, policies, labor, design, marketing, and use. Our view must be intersectional in its approaches to exigence and production, to call and response. Our view must also be multimodal in attempting to account for print, oral, visual, and performative communication and the networks within which that communication takes place—across specific modes and in transmedia spaces.

Intersectional Approaches to Technology Issues

In *Freedom Is a Constant Struggle*, Angela Davis (2016) explained that there is no way we can understand racism in any specific context, like police violence, unless we are willing to do the work to understand systemic racism, "the impact of racism on institutions *and* individual attitudes" (p. 34, emphasis added). For example, regarding the 2014 killing of Michael Brown in Ferguson, Missouri, it is crucial to link conceptually the increased militarization of policing, media proliferation of the stereotype of Black people as violent and criminal, the long history of disciplining Black bodies culminating in current mass incarceration, and the structural limits faced by even an African-American president and attorney general.

Poet Etheridge Knight (1968) anticipates these concerns in "Hard Rock Returns to Prison from the Hospital for the Criminal Insane." An unreconstructed Hard Rock, "known not to take no shit from nobody," is subjected, similar to the narrator in *Invisible Man*, to "treatment." Knight describes some of the rhetoric surrounding the event:

> The WORD / was / that Hard Rock wasn't a mean nigger
> Anymore, that doctors had bored a hole in his head,
> Cut out part of his brain, and shot electricity
> Through the rest. When they brought Hard Rock back,
> Handcuffed and chained, he was turned loose,
> Like a freshly gelded stallion, to try his new status.
> And we all waited and watched, like a herd of sheep,
> To see if the WORD was true.
>
> (p. 11)

While they wait, fellow inmates regale themselves with tales of Hard Rock's exploits. They live vicariously through him. He represents to them not criminality primarily, but Black manhood. He had been a modern incarnation of the Stagolee mythoform. However, the WORD proved to be true:

> The testing came, to see if Hard Rock was really tame.
> A hillbilly called him a black son of a bitch
> And didn't lose his teeth, a screw who knew Hard Rock
> From before shook him down and barked in his face.
> And Hard Rock did *nothing*. Just grinned and looked silly,
> His eyes empty like knot holes in a fence.

And even after we discovered that it took Hard Rock
Exactly 3 minutes to tell you his first name,
We told ourselves that he had just wised up,
Was being cool; but we could not fool ourselves for long,
And we turned away, our eyes on the ground. Crushed.
He had been our Destroyer, the doer of things
We dreamed of doing but could not bring ourselves to do,
The fears of years, like a biting whip,
Had cut deep bloody grooves
Across our backs.

(p. 12)

The potential rebels, presumably would-be challengers of White supremacy, had already been disciplined by systems of technology—schools, courts, prisons, media, labor practices—that translated into the "fears of years."

These are the overly disciplined Black bodies that authorities sought to maintain in places like Ferguson, where SWAT teams in armored vehicles confronted unarmed protesters. The military hardware was not simply technology; it was a node of decisions and actions stretching back decades about, among many things, police enforcement in Black communities, federal donations of weaponry and military gear to police departments, the demonization of Black youth in the overall public imagination, and the lack of access to jobs.

Rapper and activist Killer Mike (2014) addressed these issues directly and indirectly in pre-show remarks in St. Louis the day the grand jury announced its decision not to indict the police officer who shot Michael Brown. After speaking of his anger, frustration, and fear for his two sons, the rapper revealed passionately:

Before I came out here, there was no peace in my heart, and I wanted to walk out to burn this motherfucker down. Burn this motherfucker down. But I gotta tell you. But I gotta tell you. I'm from Atlanta, Georgia, and something said, something said, "Look for something Martin King might a said." So I Googled Martin King, and Wikipedia popped up. And he was 39 years old when you motherfuckers killed him. He was the same age as I am. The same age as El [his rap partner El-P]. He was a young man when they killed him. But I can promise you today. If I die when I walk off this stage tomorrow, I'm a let you know this: It is not about race. It is not about class. It is not about color. It is about what they killed him for. It is about poverty. It is about greed. And it is about a war machine. It is about a war machine that uses you as a battery. So I might go tomorrow. I might go the day after. But the one thing I want you to know: It is us against the motherfucking machine. Let's go!

Obviously, the flow of logic could have been smoother. Widespread poverty is about race, class, and color. But most interesting to us at this point is Killer Mike's resorting to a rhetorical tradition represented by Martin Luther King, Jr. and the technological framing of the rapper's speech, which was enabled by a quick trip to the Internet and reliant on the metaphor of "the machine."

A literal machine factors into the creation of yet another African-American mythoform, namely, John Henry, the steel driver who beat the steam drill only to die after the contest. As one ballad version of the legend depicts:

> John Henry said to his captain,
>   "A man ain't nothin' but a man,
> But before I'll let dat steam drill beat me down,
>   I'll die wid my hammer in my hand.
>   Die wid my hammer in my hand."
>
> The man that invented the steam drill
>   He thought he was mighty fine,
> John Henry drove down fourteen feet,
>   While the steam drill only made nine,
>   Steam drill only made nine.
>
> "Oh, lookaway over yonder, captain,
>   You can't see like me,"
> He gave a long and loud and lonesome cry,
>   "Lawd, a hammer be the death of me,
>   A hammer be the death of me!"
>
> John Henry had a little woman,
>   Her name was Polly Ann,
> John Henry took sick, she took his hammer,
>   She hammered like a natural man,
>   Lawd, she hammered like a natural man.
>
> John Henry hammering on the mountain
>   As the whistle blew for half-past two,
> The last words his captain heard him say,
>   "I've done hammered my insides in two,
>   Lawd, I've hammered my insides in two."
>
> The hammer that John Henry swung
>   It weighed over twelve pound,
> He broke a rib in his left hand side
>   And his intrels fell on the ground,
>   And his intrels fell on the ground.
>
> John Henry, O, John Henry,
>   His blood is running red,

Fell right down with his hammer to the ground,
Said, "I beat him to the bottom but I'm dead,
Lawd, beat him to the bottom but I'm dead.
(pp. 13–14)

The legend of John Henry has been interpreted in many ways. He has been judged to be everything from a simple, stubborn, rugged individualist who was attempting naively to delay mechanization to a sophisticated champion of workers' rights who was trying to protect jobs and preserve the humanity and dignity of fellow workers.[4] To Molefi Asante (1998),

> his [John Henry's] ability to use muscle power and physical stamina to overcome the mountain is indicative of the deep reality of the African American's reliance on physical strength during the epic sojourn in the United States. The use of the John Henry myth is usually confined to instances of physical confrontation or maintenance of philosophical positions.
>
> (p. 118)

In any case, the story has been a centerpiece of African-American folklore and has been rendered in hundreds of songs, including recordings by Harry Belafonte (1954); Big Bill Broonzy (1956); Lead Belly (1994); and Cécile McLorin Savant (2013). In addition, it has inspired or influenced literary works such as John Oliver Killens's novels *Youngblood* (1954) and *A Man Ain't Nothin' but a Man* (1975), Ernest Gaines's *Catherine Carmier* (1964) and *The Autobiography of Miss Jane Pittman* (1971), and Colson Whitehead's *John Henry Days* (2001).[5]

Often sung as a work song in addition to be being a ballad, the story of John Henry stands in the tradition of African-American folk and work songs, many of which critique labor relations. Frederick Douglass provided an example in one of his autobiographies, *My Bondage and My Freedom* (1855/1968):

"We raise de wheat,
Dey gib us de corn:
We bake de bread,
Dey gib us de cruss;
We sif de meal,
Dey gib us de huss;
We peal de meat,
Dey gib us de skin;
An dat's de way
Dey takes us in.
We skim de pot,
Dey gib us the liquor,
And say dat's good enough for nigger.
Walk over! Walk over!

> Tom butter and de fat;
> Poor nigger and you can't get over dat;
> > Walk over!"

> (pp. 252–3)

Called by Douglass a "sharp hit," the song, in his view, "is not a bad summary of the palpable injustice and fraud of slavery, giving—as it does—to the lazy and idle, the comforts which God designed should be given solely to the honest laborer" (p. 253).

Scholar Barbara Garrity-Blake (2004) illumined the complex nature of certain song production. In her study of the participation of African-American crewman in the Atlantic fish industry during the early decades of the twentieth century, she understood that their contribution was not merely labor; it was technological. As she argued, "the U.S. menhaden industry was ultimately dependent on the power of their crews' own intangible technology: the creativity, spirituality, and shared strength generated in singing" (p. 108). They reserved work songs, or chanteys, for times when they needed to lift the heaviest sets of fish. Thus, the singing provided what was tantamount to hydraulic power, enabling tasks that were not achievable without it (p. 113). But the songs were more than a means to harvest fish. They also expressed worker solidarity, resistance, and longings for better circumstances. Garrity-Blake explained, "The worksong as technology not only *functioned* as a tool to get the job done, it *signified*: the words expressed resistance to white authority, freedom to seek new wage-labor employment, and the desire to be home with loved ones" (p. 114, emphasis original). Operating within the constraints of low-wage opportunities and a segregated society, African-American crewmen nonetheless gave voice to their yearnings and critique.

Other topics that lend themselves to an intersectional rhetorical approach informed by technology include the very residential organization of Black communities. The shift to the information age and then to the Internet era has had profound effects on labor. Soul Artist Curtis Mayfield (1973) used "future shock," borrowing the title of a book by Alvin Toffler (1970). The changing employment patterns were accompanied by a drug epidemic, its worst effects spanning three decades as heroin, powder cocaine, and crack cocaine ravaged cities and rural areas that were already decimated by shifts in employment and the lack of educational equity. These conditions led to multiple forms of migration both within and beyond cities and towns, partially shaped by the growth of transportation networks, specifically automobile and air travel. This coincided with increased migration from the Caribbean and West Africa, resulting in new formations of community and understandings of Blackness. Speaking to the tensions of these concentric technological impacts and pointing to the ways that notions of family, community, and racial identity were no longer connected to physical space in the same ways they had been in prior eras, the hip-hop group De La Soul, in "Stakes Is High" (1996), offers an intriguing explanation of a common African-American semantic item: "neighborhoods are now hoods because nobody's neighbors." The group suggests that the very vocabulary of African Americans is profitably understood in intersectional terms.

Stevie Wonder as Exemplar

A particularly compelling case study of technological innovation emerged in the context of the Civil Rights and Black Power eras with the appearance of Stevie Wonder's album *Talking Book*. The entry is important in Wonder's discography for several reasons. It is seen as his first fully worked out concept album and the beginning, as he entered his early twenties, of his classic period. It is also the initial burst in the flurry of work by which he wrested from the Motown corporation creative control over his art. Because of his embrace of technological mastery and innovation as a central part of his artistic vision, Wonder technologized funk and funked up technology. He helped change the direction of funk music at a time when the Motown machine was limited in its aesthetic, and he expressed through new technology the full range of the trope of the talking book.

Released in October 1972, mere months after news of the Tuskegee syphilis experiments broke nationally and almost a year before the New York block party given by DJ Kool Herc that is widely acclaimed as the birth of hip hop, *Talking Book* was both expansive and familiar in its content and aesthetic. Its songs ranged from the ballad "You and I" played with a theremin, what was then a new-age instrument with a strange sound, to an anthem challenging listeners to let go of strongly held but irrational beliefs in "Superstition," to "Big Brother," a critique of national politics and of the Nixon administration. While other songs on the album might be seen as traditional rhythm and blues fare—songs about love, heartbreak, and hopes of new love to come—the album overall was transformative with its hard funk grooves and emphasis on electronic instrumentation. In densely layered arrangements, Wonder played multiple instruments on the album, including the aforementioned theremin, a Fender Rhodes electric piano, a Moog bass, and a Hohner clavinet. The overall sound of the album developed through Wonder's collaboration with producers and engineers Bob Margouleff and Malcolm Cecil at Electric Lady studio, previously known as the artistic home of Jimi Hendrix. Wonder worked with Margouleff and Cecil on a synthesizer system known as TONTO, or The Original New Timbral Orchestra. TONTO was a huge sonic laboratory, with synthesizers, circuits, patches, and wires everywhere. In this environment, Wonder merged technology, funk, and messages of racial justice and Black pride. As Margouleff (2012) noted,

> his music making superseded the entertainment business. His music reflected the cry for civil rights, the urban Black experience, and about who he was. I felt like his music was very political . . . he didn't just write love songs, but he related to the world's reality at that time. I thought he was a messenger.

With *Talking Book*, Wonder presented a clear articulation of Blackness that spoke to all of American culture but specifically to Black people, an articulation that was built on a particular mix of individual freedom, exploration, mastery, and innovation with technologies as well as a deep and abiding love for Black people and an understanding of literacy as liberation work. *Talking Book* was not just a cool title for an album or merely a set of reflections on oral traditions in song, but a funk sermon and a masterful reworking of the talking-book trope for the computer age. Wonder not only made the talking book talk to him, but he talked back to it and through it created his own "book" and made it talk to both Black people and the larger nation. In the process, he demonstrated that technologies do not only have to be weapons of war or instruments of domination, but could also be deployed for racial justice and as part of a broad humanism linking audiences across boundaries.

As indicated in Chapter 2, the trope of the talking book/silent book marks a quest for literacy and liberation by oppressed Black subjects. Gronniosaw and Equiano grab hold of the word and become able to wield it for their purposes. In his monograph *The Talking Book*, Allen Dwight Callahan (2008) viewed this activity to be divinely inspired and connected to the biblical story of the Apostle Paul's miraculous release from prison. Those who learned to read often found themselves called to preach as well. Because the preacher's authority to preach was often grounded in the miraculous revelation of The Book, the preacher's very work represented liberation on multiple levels: the individual freedom (often including literal freedom from slavery) acquired by the preaching man or woman, and that preacher's charge to lead others. The trope connects Black oral traditions to the acquisition of print literacies beyond the Bible, with many people using memorization and griotic storytelling traditions in their "reading" of the text that enabled further instruction that led to their learning to read and write. The oral tradition served as both evidence of literacy and bridge to it, keeping both linked even until today.

William W. Cook, in his 1993 essay "Writing in the Spaces Left," wrote about the mandate of literacy for freedom and the centrality of the talking-book trope to this effort:

> To preach the word demands possession of that word, and such possession is predicated on seizing for the creating and speaking self spaces not yet claimed by the texts of the dominant discourse.... Ours is not a foreclosed narrative or a narrative of foreclosure. There are still spaces left.
>
> (pp. 24–5)

Cook helps us to expand the trope as we shift the frame of reference from slave narratives to contemporary times. The modern talking book can thus be seen as:

1. The collective "book" of oral texts in the tradition that become a literal talking book: tales, sermons, poems, speeches, spirituals, blues, hip hop, and more.

2. The range of alternative texts, networks, practices, and spaces for literacy work that allows Black people to acquire and employ literacies on their own terms and for their own purposes.
3. The newly freed person and collectives of people talking back to and/or rewriting the book—reinterpreting and often transforming its messages and interpretations in ways that reflect Black priorities and epistemologies.

Talking Book invokes the talking-book trope—and is its literal instantiation. It has contributed to a rising Black techno-dialogic. In fact, Afrofuturism, a discourse in which Wonder has a secure place, itself is a form of the talking-book trope at work, a hacking of narratives and systems of code that can rewrite human existence, not only through academic discourse, but certainly in and through it. In this way, African-American rhetoric as a field of study is an Afrofuturist project, and Afrofuturism is deeply connected to the study of African-American rhetoric. The field must include, but move beyond, micro-level concerns about how people use technologies to innovate. In addition to these important explorations, it must also take up the questions of how Black people have attempted to navigate the terrain, to influence the terms, on which human relationships with technologies are negotiated. The ways in which large-scale debates about science and technologies bear on Black lives are just as important to the study of rhetoric as questions of delivery when former President Barack Obama did or did not use a teleprompter as he gave speeches or how the "clapback" developed as a specific rhetorical form in online discourse. Stevie Wonder, as a musical artist and later technology innovator and technology advocate for the blind, will remain central to such investigation.[6]

Digital Divides

The seeming ubiquitous presence of digital devices and connections makes it easy to assume that digital divides either no longer exist or are no longer significant factors in access to opportunity or quality of life for groups of people who have been subjected to systematic exclusion from the technology sector. However, ongoing, systematic digital divides remain and continue to exacerbate interconnecting forms of inequality that mark African-American life. Even as cellular phones, computers, and Internet connections seem universal, there are still gaps in Internet access.

In any event, having the tools and means to use the Internet is only the most basic element of access. Knowledge of how to use and maximize one's use in line with one's goals and objectives; meaningful experiences with and within any kind of technological system from use to labor to design to leadership to ownership; knowledge of issues related to the use of any technological tool or system to enable individuals and communities to make informed decisions about balancing use, critique and resistance; the ability to deploy technologies toward meaningful individual and collective goals; and employment and ownership within the technology sector, where the stubbornness of the digital divide endures, are all crucial elements of access. The staggering amounts of money it takes to have any kind of successful product launch alone makes it difficult for people of color to have anywhere near an even playing field when it comes to owning technology sector products, platforms, and companies. Attempts to attract venture capital from those who do have finances to invest have been highly stratified by race as well. We can only guess at how different the Internet and the broader technology sector would be, two decades after the popularization of the World Wide Web, if the needs, preferences, priorities, and potential contributions of African Americans, Latinx, and Indigenous people participated in these spheres at rates even half of their proportions in the nation's population. Further, we can only imagine the innovations with individual technologies and the kinds of change the whole technology sector might see if the needs, priorities, and perspectives of people of color were taken seriously in STEM fields and funding processes.

Of course, this lack of regard for the prospects of Black innovation is not unique to technologies or digital culture, but it has very specific valences in these contexts. One reason that narratives of enduring digital divides are such difficult topics within Black scholarship is that no matter how deeply embedded and enduring those divides are, devoting attention to them runs the risk of another deeply embedded problem: the stereotype of Black people as inherently non-technological. As we have shown, this is far from the case.

Digital Innovation

A significant element of what led so many people to see the Internet as a transformative achievement in communications technology is in the ways that it pronounced a dramatic shift from broadcast modes of communication to "here comes everybody," to invoke the title of Clay Shirky's 2008 book on organizing in a digitally connected world. This suggests an African-American digital rhetoric that links technology experts and lay users and gives importance both to organized struggles for justice and everyday living. Examples of how this combination can play out in an African-American digital rhetoric abound: the ongoing strategies and appeals being invented, debated, negotiated, and employed in the Movement for Black Lives and #BlackLivesMatter; the social media strategies of media personalities like Jamilah Lemieux, former editor at Ebony.com and current Vice President of News and Men's Programming for Interactive One; sportswriter and media analyst Bomani Jones; the ongoing digital presence of groups like the Crunk Feminist Collective; specific communities of interest on spaces like Tumblr, YouTube, and WordPress; everyday interactions on Twitter and SnapChat; and how people communicate in the most everyday settings through group texts and chats. These examples only begin to show the range of what students and scholars in African-American digital rhetoric might explore.

Notes

1. For an analysis of the broad impact of the cotton gin on slavery and the growth of the cotton industry, see Christopher Hamner's "The Disaster of Innovation" (2012).
2. See, respectively, Muhammad's *Message to the Blackman in America* (1973, pp. 290–1; Malcolm X's, "God's Judgment of White America," (1971, p. 131); and Alejandro Rojas' article, "Farrakhan Asks President Obama to Open Area 51 and Reveal Its UFO Secrets" (2014). The example from Malcolm X does not represent the fully formed argument, but he does speak of divine retribution, White doom, the lake of fire, and asserts, "death and divine destruction hang at this very moment in the skies over America" (p. 131).
3. This notion was so prevalent that the National Negro Congress was moved to counter the sentiment in the aftermath of the attack of the Japanese military on Pearl Harbor. In the pamphlet *The Negro Will Defend America*, the Congress equated fascism in Japan with that in Germany and Italy.
4. For a discussion of the continuum poles relative to the legend of John Henry, see Keith Gilyard's *John Oliver Killens* (2010, pp. 286–8). Killens's politically astute, proletarian hero, who promotes ethnic alliances, is contrasted to Ezra Jack Keats's 1965 *John Henry*, which is a relatively apolitical tale and virtually silent on racial issues.
5. In *Youngblood*, twenty-one years before the publication of *John Henry*, Killens modeled Joe Youngblood after the folk hero. For connections between the legend of John Henry and Gaines's fiction, see Keith Byerman's *Fingering the Jagged Grain* (1985, pp. 68, 89).
6. Wonder's work with technologies went far beyond his use of them as a musical artist. Throughout the 1970s, he collaborated with Robert Moog on future versions of the Moog synthesizer, including work as a paid endorser. He went on to collaborate with Ray Kurzweil to help design assistive and adaptive technologies for the vision impaired. In 2009 he was named a UN Messenger of Peace, a platform he used to advocate for accessibility issues and for people with disabilities. In a 2013 meeting of the UN General Assembly on disability and development, he used his own story—his own development of literacies and knowledge about how to move in the world and succeed as an unsighted person—to advocate for greater accessibility of adaptive tools and technologies for people around the world. He called for substantial investment by member nations in subsidizing adaptive technologies so that people "will be more independent and feel freer" ("Statement delivered by Stevie Wonder").

6   Rhetoric and Black Twitter

In late October 2016, a major roast took place on Twitter after Peter Howell, writing for the *Toronto Star* about the movie *Moonlight* (Romanski, 2016), mistakenly identified the linguistic phenomenon of code switching as "coat switching." The mistake was a fairly innocuous one, as Howell defined the activity as "shifting cultural traits and vernacular to suit different circumstances"—not a bad definition—and praised Barry Jenkins' work directing *Moonlight* as being guided by a refusal to feature such maneuvering. Indeed, part of what made the movie resonate so fully with an expansive audience is that in its authenticity it refused to privilege the ever-present White gaze that exists in media generally, and Hollywood films specifically.

Despite Howell's rather harmless verbal misstep, amusement still ensued among Black users on Twitter as the full range of their signifyin power and a strong undercurrent of call-and-response combined to make the hashtag trend, with the term "coatswitching" resonating as a joke for people in and beyond the virtual community of Black Twitter users. Several months later a user with the screen name "Ol Querty Bastard" (@TheDILLon1) posted the following tweet of a GIF image of former President Barack Obama, Beyoncé, and Jay-Z morphing from a regular picture of the three to one that is lightened, with the #coatswitching hashtag, to cue up and include it in that prior conversation (Figure 6.1).

This moment stands out in Twitter lore for its Black users because beyond poking innocent—if raucous—fun at a major newspaper's mistaken identification of a practice so widely discussed among Black people and so widely studied among linguists of all backgrounds, the moment showed the full range of why the use of Twitter by Blacks is the object of so much attention by observers—many of whom are not Black. "How Black People Use Twitter," to cue a 2010 article by Farhad Manjoo published on Slate.com, has been an ongoing subject of curiosity and confusion, of appreciation and appropriation, by news media, pop culture aficionados, scholars, public commentators, and everyday people. In that ongoing comedic roast, Black users of Twitter offered a public challenge to media that are inattentive to the depths and nuances of Black culture and did so with a complete refusal to code switch—a complete refusal to perform for a White gaze, whether a White media gaze or the gaze of White and other non-Black Twitter users.

Figure 6.1

These communication choices and practices have resulted in the phenomenon known as #BlackTwitter, one that is at once communal for those users who participate in it and a known driver of both content and traffic on and beyond Twitter itself. As such, #BlackTwitter is one of the most promising spaces for understanding the combinations and intersections at work in African-American digital rhetoric. It is a space that is at once amorphous yet clearly discernible. It is public, counterpublic, and underground. It crosses the entire continuum between public address and deliberation for broad communal goals and the most everyday and vernacular kinds of communication. An exploration of the rhetorical principles and practices employed by those who participate in the network shows that Black Twitter is a site that is as rich and important as the lyceum, debate hall, Black church, beauty shop, barbershop, and Black music tradition. As a response to the rhetorical challenges attending Black life in the twenty-first century, #BlackTwitter reveals its users, similar to the "permanent persuader" of Antonio Gramsci (1971, p. 10), to be persistent persuaders for whom rhetorical engagement happens constantly, on multiple levels, in every tweet, conversation thread, and communicative act. This ongoing rhetorical work demonstrates community building happening in real time, opposition to continued forms of racialized oppression, and, significantly, an intentional claiming of and holding onto joy as an act of resistance.

Launched in 2006 as a short messaging service inviting users to share chatter-like status messages by asking "what are you doing?," Twitter has become a vexed yet crucial space for public conversation the world over, with the site claiming more than 300 million users in 2016. Black Twitter was recognized as a distinct marvel drawing curiosity and media attention as early as 2009, and it has been the subject of sustained media and scholarly attention ever since. In 2015, the *Los Angeles Times* hired Dexter Thomas to cover Black Twitter as a beat in the same way that a reporter would cover the arts or metro news or politics. Other media attention has been more focused on how Black users of Twitter generally, and #BlackTwitter as a happening in particular, have exerted outsized influence on broad media trends. Black Entertainment Television (BET), part of the Viacom media conglomerate, announced in April 2017 that it would partner with Twitter to launch a study of Black Twitter with a focus on top Twitter hashtags and a "convergence culture" kind of look at social watching—people coming together on Twitter to live tweet television shows and other major events. Because of the bountiful discussion generated by the announcement, including concerns about marketing interests, BET published a revised statement to its site on May 22, 2017, explaining that the study, rather than look primarily at Black Twitter users' engagement with the site as a way of studying media consumption and thus patterns that could be used to attract advertisers, was essentially about "shining a light on Black Twitter" and demonstrating its power and potential in forwarding in the public domain the agendas of African Americans.

Scholarly attention to Black Twitter has explored a wide range of topics and concerns, from identity construction and performance (Florini, 2014) to digital protest and advocacy in social movements to end street harassment and police violence (Bonilla and Rosa, 2015; Sherri Williams, 2015) to the ways that Black Twitter provides a fertile space for linguistic examinations of African-American Vernacular English (Jones, 2014) to how the specific affordances of Twitter contribute to constructions of race by way of the viral spread of cultural content (Sharma, 2013). Moreover, as one would expect, there is a wide-ranging set of conversations in both scholarly outlets and public media about the degree to which online activism and advocacy is meaningful or contributes to "real" social change. In short, #BlackTwitter is an ongoing cultural conversation that combines features of well-known rhetorical sites like the beauty shop, lyceum, studio, soapbox, and activist rally. Furthermore, it is a prime example of what Ron Eglash (2004) identifies as "vernacular technology" at work (p. vii). In this case, Black technology use is one of "many instances in which [lay users] reinvent these products and rethink these knowledge systems, often in ways that embody critique, resistance, or outright revolt" (p. vii).

Part of what makes Black Twitter fascinating, yet perplexing, to many is the fact that it is an amorphous, constantly shifting presence on Twitter that, despite its obvious impact, cannot be fully defined. There is no membership, no appointed time when people show up. Individual Black people might use Twitter in many ways that include participation in #BlackTwitter. On the other hand, not all Black people who use Twitter, whether in the United States, Canada, or anywhere else in the African diaspora would see themselves as part of Black Twitter, and there is no set of characteristics that reliably could be ascribed to users who do. Meredith Clark (2014), author of the first dissertation devoted to Black Twitter, in an interview with *The Atlantic* titled "The Truth About Black Twitter," defines it as "a temporally linked group of connectors that share culture, language and interest, and talking about specific topics with a Black frame of reference . . . not just limited to US Blacks, but Blacks throughout the diaspora" (Ramsey, 2015). For Clark's definition, it is the common "frame of reference" that is crucial to collective Black experiences on the site. While analyses of Black Twitter often focus on content and language through examinations of trending topics, hashtags, debates, and forms of advocacy, the specific discursive elements and rhetorical practices employed by these connectors who share so much are key to understanding why Black Twitter is so durable and innovative, and why it can maintain a communal element particular to a Black frame of reference while being the object of so much curiosity and, at times, outright appropriation.

To understand Black Twitter as central to African-American rhetoric in the twenty-first century is to understand that folklore and the epistemological frameworks of lay technology users in everyday contexts matters at least as much as the formal address of a university president or the design of a software interface. Such an approach to rhetoric has been presented and detailed by the authors on multiple prior occasions (Gilyard, 1996, 2011; Banks, 2006, 2011) as well as in this present volume. Everyday posts and interactions by Black Twitter users show that the site is at once a hush harbor,[1] a lyceum, a public square, and a space for counterpublic, vernacular interrogations and interventions that have become at least as important to Black rhetoric as the activist rally, the church, and literary movements have been, especially in a context in which dramatic shifts in physical community have led to correlating changes in the physical institutions that were such important sites of rhetorical production. For some of its users, Black Twitter has become a communal space that allows for connections with people that augment some of what is lost with various kinds of migration and displacement. While Clark identified content and a common frame of reference as important elements of Black Twitter, it is the "hidden transcript" that its users bring to the space that allows it to fulfill so many functions that drive both cultural and digital innovation and a communal experience. To grasp how users create a communal space that fills so many functions and somehow remain hidden in plain view despite greater cultural exchange and appropriation requires attention to the discursive practices and rhetorical dimensions that make up the common frame of reference that Clark discussed. The richness of the space, how it operates between invisibility and hypervisibility, between explicit, organized efforts at persuasion and everyday, folkloric kinds of communication, marks Black Twitter as an example of what we might call "convergence rhetorics" at work.

Just as ever more multiple functions and purposes have become part of our digital tools and networks, as our "smart" phones function as telephones, audio studios, mail centers, video booths, multimedia libraries, hubs for online social interaction, and more, so have multiple functions and purposes proliferated in cyber-rhetorical spaces. #BlackTwitter as a rhetorical and communal space takes on functions of the church, the public arena, the soapbox, the studio, the corner, the hip-hop cipher, the gathering place for small collectives, and more. Of course, this has become the case for many social media spaces, irrespective of particular racial, ethnic, or cultural exigencies and experiences. But the key to understanding how Black Twitter coheres as such a distinct space within a site that was designed to foster the most immediate and ephemeral kinds of communication depends on understanding the specific history, discursive forms, and rhetorical practices that shape Black Twitter as a cultural and political formation.

Some Informal Black Social Media History

When examining #BlackTwitter, it is crucial that we don't commit what could be called the Jes Grew fallacy: making the assumption that a new phenomenon or critical departure emerged out of nowhere.[2] It is not only true that the discursive strategies we see employed by legions of Black Twitter users emerge from a centuries-old set of rhetorical traditions and practices; they also emerge from a history of online use and online communities that stretches back more than twenty years, since the Graphical User Interface (GUI) led to the creation of new possibilities for online interaction. This history is marked by significant Black participation and innovation.

With regard to origins, we might humorously trace the beginning of Black social media to CB radio users, a development treated in "Breaker, Breaker," an episode of the TV sitcom *Good Times* in 1977 (Monte). In this episode, the main character J.J. starts to interact with people on a recently purchased CB. His younger brother Michael becomes curious, starts to use the radio, and unwittingly becomes the first documented example of a "catfish:" someone who on a social network intentionally or unintentionally misleads another user whom they have never met offline. The catfish moment of Michael flirting with another young person on the network is far less important than the fact that the show portrays Black people looking to CB radio as a means to communicate and find community beyond the boundaries of their Chicago neighborhood, and in ways that are rooted in Black vernacular and style.

Some of the antecedents to #BlackTwitter in online history after the introduction of the GUI include Yahoo and AOL chat rooms dedicated to African Americans, NetNoir/TalkCity, BlackPlanet, MySpace, Friendster, and OkayPlayer. Contemporaneous with Twitter have been Facebook, Ning, Vine, and Instagram. Black culture and discourse flourished in all of these spaces.

Masked, Hushed, Unmasked, and Hyperbolic

Masking, for both survival and rhetorical purposes, is so ingrained into Black life and cultures, especially in the United States, as to not need much in the way of explanation. From Paul Laurence Dunbar's poem "We Wear the Mask" (1895/1993) to "The Mask" by the Fugees (1996), the idea of keeping some language, some ideas, some styles, and some spaces "hushed" is a central theme throughout literary, public, and popular cultures. The centrality of masking leads to rhetorical practices of using both silence and double- or multiply-voiced ways of communicating that enable single utterances or uses of an image or link or video or meme to convey multiple levels of meaning and thereby serve multiple purposes for multiple audiences. Masking and/or signifyin can preserve just enough indeterminacy for important parts of a message to miss audiences for whom it is not intended. Masking and signifyin are absolutely critical to #BlackTwitter's existence and its ability to operate as a culturally relevant space for its participants, especially when it's common knowledge that the "tweets is watchin."

Signifyin as a discursive or rhetorical practice depends on an understanding that communication is subject to intertextual "play," shaded levels of critique and/or ritualized dissing—from the literally playful and jovial to the utterly serious. There is joy and a communal element to engaging in the game itself. In her 2006 book *Word From the Mother*, Geneva Smitherman informed or reminded us of the old saying, "signification is the nigga's occupation" (p. 70). Various kinds of signifyin play, or ritual performances, place a premium on spontaneity. Smitherman's description of one kind of signifyin, the Dozens, is relevant to understanding what exists as a continual art form within #BlackTwitter, whether the topic is current events, organized protests, gender dynamics, or awards shows. As she wrote, "one upmanship is the goal of this oral contest, best played in a group of appreciative onlookers, who are secondary participants in the game. They provide a kind of running commentary, repeating a really clever dis or interjecting responses . . . [t]he audience, with its laughter, high fives and other responses, pushes the verbal duel to greater and greater heights of oratorical fantasy" (2000, p. 224). It is important to indicate here that while public awareness of signifyin is often limited to versions of jokes and games, it involves much more and is often a part of serious discourse with and among Black speakers. Claudia Mitchell-Kernan noted the more serious function of signifyin in her 1972 essay "Signifying, Loud-Talking and Marking": "[s]ignifying, however, also refers to a way of encoding messages or meanings which involves, in most cases, an element of indirection" (p. 315). This indirection, and sometimes misdirection, expressed both verbally and nonverbally, linguistically and extralinguistically, enables veiled critique in situations where more explicit critique might invite overt persecution or other negative consequences.

Signifyin as rhetorical practice takes place in conjunction with call-and-response so that any conversation among Black people on the site, whether they happen to be tweeting from South Africa, Haiti, Germany, Kenya, or any other nation can become a larger communal exchange not limited to individual replies to individual tweets. In this way, topics (whether they congeal around hashtags or not, whether they become trending or not) can become virtual and partly veiled public rallies, congregations, stand-up comedy sessions, or living rooms.

But masking and signifyin are one end of a very wide spectrum. Black discourse, from toasting traditions and bragging games, up through hip hop, trap, and bounce, is also about the outlandish, the extreme, the hyperbolic. Just as survival depended (and still depends) on the ability to tell necessary truths on lower registers, the ability to laugh, boast, and even lie in loud voices as irreverently as one can imagine has been just as crucial to African-American communication. Just as Br'er Rabbit and the Signifying Monkey are archetypical examples of trickster figures who survive by misdirection and outwitting more powerful opponents, there is the outlandish, transgressive Stagolee. This latter figure has lived on through blues singers such as Ma Rainey, Bessie Smith, and Billie Holiday, the artists that Angela Davis profiles in *Blues Legacies and Black Feminism* (1999), and the Stagolee mythoform has continued to be represented by the likes of Betty Mabry Davis, Millie Jackson, Lil Kim, and Nicki Minaj. On Twitter, we recognize this trait in rhetorical exemplars like Feminista Jones and Jamilah Lemieux.

Black Twitter users individually and collectively refuse to mute conversation on topics that outsiders might view as objectionable, and they refuse to avoid internal conversation and in-group critique simply because that might put "dirty laundry" or "family business" on display. Full-throated critiques of the "politics of respectability"[3] are a regular feature of the current dialogue. Black Twitter users often refuse to mask certain elements of individual lives or communal experiences to be viewed as palatable to outsiders. From content to form, loudness, laughter, and exaggeration are found in measures at least equal to muting and indirection. The hyperbolic is just as vital as the hush harbor. To put it another way, whereas rhetoric was once widely seen, to paraphrase Quintilian, as the "good wo/man speaking well,"[4] Black rhetoric, especially as manifested on Black Twitter, insists that the "bad wo/man who says what some of you are scared to say" is crucial, too. For every smooth figure like former President Barack Obama, who was well practiced in understatement, there is a Congresswoman Maxine Waters who will fearlessly lay it all on the line.

One way that the hyperbolic is marked within Black Twitter is in the descriptor, sometimes the exclamation that someone, or some people, or Black Twitter as a whole (or some component of it) has NO CHILL. Sometimes this is used as a hashtag appended to wild tweets or conversations, and sometimes it is tossed into the stream of tweets as a declaration, sometimes in complaint, but often in celebration. The expression has made its way beyond Black Twitter into general popular culture usage, but is also related to expressions like *flatline*, *I'm dead* (now also expressed in emoticon form as well as in various images, GIFs, and memes). The common exaggerations of expressions like *laughing out loud*, *laughing my behind off*, *crying laughing*, and others get taken to their fullest hyperbolic extreme.

Some of this activity has become part of Black Twitter lore, touchstones that lead to rhetorical commonplaces for future conversations. Infamous, outlandish moments like #Temecula or a twitter novella chronicled as a #Zola story or "regional slander"—moments when entire cities or regions get roasted—comprise one end of the spectrum.[5] Some instantiations are far more serious, from advocacy and activism campaigns like #YouOKSis and #BlackTransLivesMatter and #iftheygunnedmedown. And some are everyday, even ritualistic kinds of collective performances that have transformed the social-watching phenomenon. All of these conversations and campaigns, from the serious to the silly and in between, demonstrate the wide range from the hushed to the hyperbolic and how the uses of signifyin and call-and-response transform masses of individual interactions and weak ties, like retweets, link shares, and reply tweets, into powerful communal spaces, even when notions of community are fraught, amorphous, and changing. The wide continuum from the hushed to the hyperbolic also includes some rhetorical forms or practices that are either specific to Black Twitter or play out in specific ways within Black Twitter.

The THIS!!!!!!!

Social media cultures depend on the ability of users to share content beyond their own posts, so it is natural that specific discursive practices would attend the linking, retweeting, or other kinds of sharing of content on Twitter. One of the many ways that people who participate in Black Twitter share content in ways that build the broader communal experience is through what we are (somewhat playfully) identifying as the THIS!!!!!, or hyperbolic forms of expressed affirmation that are a crucial component of sharing other people's content. As opposed to merely retweeting an item or posting a link, many users will sometimes offer enthusiastic, expressed affirmation in the sharing. When this happens, the repost or retweeted item becomes an occasion not only to express identification with the content, but with the person or networks who either created the content or also shared it. The THIS!!!!! expresses an affinity with that person and the larger collective. Often this affirmation and enthusiasm are communicated in exactly this form: the word *this*, sometimes in caps, and any number of exclamation points accompanying it.

The Roast or Drag

Roasts and *drags* are related but distinct forms of signifyin sessions, during which a person or company or organization might be joked about mercilessly by groups of users. Known by a range of other names—snapping, cappin, joanin, the previously mentioned Dozens, or roasting—ritualized verbal contests built on jokes and humorous insults have long been documented as a traditional form of Black discourse. On Black Twitter, whether a roast—sometimes also referred to as slander—is initiated by an individual or initiated as a collective exercise, the event is sometimes far more about the users themselves than the people being joked about. One such moment when the roast was playful and even loving, revolves around what is known as the #UncleDenzel meme.

The Uncle Denzel meme came into existence in May 2015, when Oscar award-winning actor Denzel Washington was photographed at the fight between Floyd Mayweather and Manny Pacquiao. The photo of an unshaven, scruffy Washington in a blue tracksuit and Black baseball cap appeared to have caught him in conversation, at an angle and with a look that is far from the image of the dashing, ultra-polished Hollywood leading man that has been his dominant persona in over thirty years of movie and television acting. The photograph went viral almost instantly and became a meme within Black Twitter known as #UncleDenzel, becoming the subject of innumerable jokes and related hashtags to such an extent that Uncle Denzel can now be seen as enduring a character as Washington has ever portrayed on film. Washington himself seemed surprised and at least mildly irked by all of the jokes that were seemingly at his expense. In an interview with *Global Grind*, he responded to a question about the meme as if those making the jokes were "haters" jealous of his success:

> If I had my wallet, I'd show it to you, because they didn't know what I was doing . . . they don't need to know. Those who can, do. Those who can't talk about those who can. I'm gonna say it again—send that out: those who can, do. Those who can't talk about those who can. Now can you? Or can you not? Are you one of those who just sits on the sideline and talk about other people, or can you step up?
>
> (BlogXilla, 2016)

It appears that while Washington was aware of the meme and the way it went viral, he was unaware of the playful nature of the voluminous comments, jokes, and posts. Even through the hashtag, #UncleDenzel, the meme and all the posts connected to it show that the very reason it went viral was because of how the photograph humanized Washington in ways that his Hollywood image could not. Through his movies and impromptu inspirational speeches and advocacy campaigns for organizations like the Boys and Girls Clubs, Denzel Washington is someone to be admired: handsome, intelligent, polished, philanthropic, action hero, idol of women, and more. #UncleDenzel is just that—your down-to-earth uncle rooted in Black traditions of fictive kinship. Uncle Denzel instantly became the elder asking if someone's mother was home, if he could fix their car engine, and as someone who would use vernacular aphorisms like "big bank take little bank." So while the jokes seemed merciless from those outside of #BlackTwitter, the roast was one done in love, poking huge fun at a megastar's expense, but ultimately claiming him as part of an extended fictive family.

The *drag* differs from the roast not so much in form but in intent. One way to understand a Black Twitter dragging is as a collective *clapback*, or stern retort. These moments, sometimes short, sometimes extended, take place when a person or event conveners or people participating in a conversation have erred so egregiously that they are roasted with a significant critical edge. A Black Twitter drag might target Black people or non-Black people, and it takes on varying degrees of harshness depending on the perceived offense. Sexist and homophobic actions or behaviors are often subjects that might get someone dragged inside of Black Twitter. Overt or insidious expressions of racism or interlocking kinds of bias across race, sex, gender, and class might get a non-Black person dragged. Rapper Meek Mill, actors Matt Damon, Stacey Dash, and Raven Symone have all been dragged on occasion, as has well-known chef and television personality Paula Deen. Hollywood itself, the Academy of Motion Picture Arts and Sciences, and the Oscar Awards, are regularly panned through the hashtag #OscarsSoWhite, created by Twitter user @ReignofApril.

The Clapback

One way in which humor—especially signifyin humor—becomes central to discursive resistance among those who participate in Black Twitter is, as indicated, *the clapback*. The clapback is a witty and incisive rejoinder, but it has become a rhetorical form unto itself. One point of origin for the term is a 2003 song of the same name by hip-hop artist Ja Rule. In a hyperbolic—and hypermasculine—style, the song's lyrics show the persona insisting that he (and his crew) will respond aggressively to any threats that might meet them. If you clap, "we gon clap back." The song presents the fact of the clapback as a certainty and therefore a warning. On Twitter, the act of shooting back referenced in the song becomes metaphorical. The clapback is a form of signifyin that whether playful or serious has a hard edge that acts as a warning: retreat or this could get (discursively) ugly. The clapback is interruption, intervention, and correction, immediately, on time and in real time.

One of the clearest examples of how this Black Twitter-specific retort operates and has reached communal recognition as a form of its own can be found in a hashtag that began in 2015 but became an ongoing roast and remains a touchstone conversation and signifier in its own right, #ThanksgivingClapback. In this instant-classic hashtag, created by Twitter user @KashmirVIII, many of those who post use imagined conversations with family to laugh at the family anxieties or conflicts that often infuse holiday gatherings, to respond to generational criticisms from elders, and to have fun with representations of cultural patterns, tropes, and debates. It became a broader Internet sensation with lists of top tweets shared on sites like Awesomely Luvvie, Hello Beautiful, Vibe Magazine, BuzzFeed, and Mashable. Twitter accounts threaded people's favorite examples, and accounts and posts proliferated on Tumblr, Pinterest, and Reddit as well. The hashtag is connected to others like #ThanksgivingWithBlackFamilies and #ThanksgivingWithCaribbeanFamilies, and the content ranges from text only to layered multimedia tweets with image-based memes, Vine video loops, GIFs, and more. While the themes of the tweets associated with this threaded conversation are too voluminous to analyze here, one major theme is a rejection of limited—and limiting—understandings of family, relationships, and individual identity that are often part of popular critiques of respectability politics.

https://twitter.com/JackeeHarry/status/669314848195551232

Figure 6.2

An example from famed television actor and clapback aficionado Jackée Harry shows a tame, but pointed version, punning on the definition of "child" to poke fun at the idea that children ought to be served first at holiday meals. Some examples are more merciless, including this one by user @jay11adams that imagines a clapback correcting an overly nosy aunt:

https://twitter.com/jay11adams/status/669298077430358016

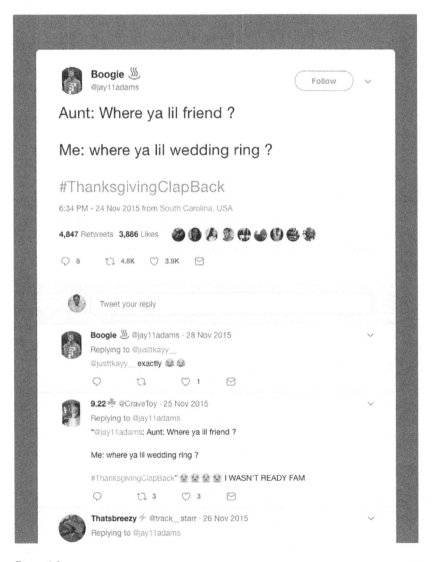

Figure 6.3

Cultural analyst and comedian Luvvie Ajayi (2015) talks about the hashtag and the role of humor online on her blog Awesomely Luvvie. The use of humor online, and the kinds of communal joy that emerges from the call-and-response nature of huge collectives of people joining in on a conversation like this, "serves as distraction" in an environment that constantly bombards users with the specter of Black death and atrocities visited on Black people that lead to both outrage and resignation, action and inaction. She describes this particular hashtag as another example of "laughing to keep from crying."

The clapback also serves a more serious role in individual and collective use on Black Twitter. The form has become part of the multiply layered ways people defend themselves from being targeted by hostile trolls. Black women, Queer, and LGBT people are targeted in disturbingly vicious ways: trolls and abusers seek them out by picture, user name, hashtag, or other keywords in order to attack their opinions, language, ideas, looks, and identities. This broader problem of online abuse, including the particular homophobic, sexist, and racist ways Black people are targeted, has been such a problem for Twitter that multiple attempts to sell the site and thus procure more funding for its growth have failed due to the inability to curb this abuse. A 2016 article by Robinson Meyer in *The Atlantic* titled "Twitter's Famous Racist Problem" detailed just how broad and deep these problems were, and a Newsweek piece by Marc Perton, "Why Doesn't Anyone Want to Buy Twitter?" suggested that weak responses to online abuse factored into the decision of prospective buyers like Google, Disney, and Salesforce not to acquire the company.

Rhetorical Situations and Cautionary Notes

Even with its vibrancy, then, life on Black Twitter is fraught with serious problems. As stated, Black people are sometimes targeted in ways ranging from the erasure of Black voices and concerns to obnoxious trolling and threats of violence. In addition to these forms of discursive erasure and violence is the fact that Black Twitter conversations, language, and trends are always being watched and mined for copy/paste content and stories for news sites and traditional news media. These individuals and companies may be seen as "culture vultures"— people who actively profit from repackaging the language, memes, and references of Black Twitter for broader circulation. In this way, Black digital cultures are subject to the same kinds of policing and appropriation (and genuine exchange and influence) of the blues, hip hop, and activist movements of prior eras. This means that there is no such thing as solely Black conversation to be had in public spaces online, or even within public view, whether that conversation is serious or lighthearted, directed at broader audiences or desiring to be left alone.

Simone Browne (2015) identifies Blackness itself as an object of intense surveillance in public spaces and beyond. Beginning her study with Frantz Fanon's observations about the "night and day surveillance"[6] (p. 6) of Black bodies, then building on the work of Black-feminist scholars and writers such as Toni Cade Bambara and Angela Davis, Browne shows how racialized surveillance constructs boundaries along racial lines, reifies race, and often promotes discriminatory and violent treatment (p. 8).

This constant surveillance of Blackness in the space of Twitter involves both discursive violence directed at Black users and continued appropriation, erasure, and theft of content. It is an ongoing joke among Black Twitter users that trending topics on #BlackTwitter today will be compiled in articles on sites like Mashable and Buzzfeed tomorrow. Some cases of appropriation and outright erasure persist and speak to large tensions in digital cultures that have been at work since the earliest eras of the Internet: a communitarian ethos of sharing vs. intellectual property and commercialization, and the viability of Black cultures in online spaces designed and built with little involvement by Black people or attention to Black interests. Some of these cases have been about lack of attribution when a concept tied to a hashtag takes off and reaches viral status: #OscarsSoWhite, created by April Reign, and #BlackLivesMatter, co-created by Alicia Garza, Patrice Cullors, and Opal Tometi, are examples of this kind of erasure. Fortunately, each of these creators has countered the erasure of their contributions and now frequently are credited, if still not always, by writers and commenters.

Emma Gray Ellis (2017), writing for *Wired* magazine, examined the economic impact of erasure by considering the popularization of the phrase "on fleek," created by a Vine user named Kayla Lewis (aka Peaches Monroee). Lewis used the phrase to describe her exquisitely styled eyebrows, and the phrase became a meme in its own right and a viral sensation on Twitter and other social media platforms. In this case, the erasure of Lewis's creation was not just about lack of attribution as the meme went viral. As Ellis explained, this erasure was compounded by the fact that major companies began to use the meme to advertise their products and sell their brands. After detailing some of those companies and the commercial reach of Monroee's phrase, Ellis (2017) drew the following conclusion:

> why didn't she get access to college scholarships like Chewbacca Mom, whose claim to fame boils down to laughing while wearing a plastic mask? Lewis's problem is part intellectual property law, part access to influence, and all systemic racial inequalities. However egalitarian the Internet was supposed to be, creatives' ability to profit off their viral content seems to depend on race.

Ellis, citing K J Greene from the Thomas Jefferson School of Law, went on to illuminate that Black content influences and even drives digital culture in ways very similar to hip hop over the last several decades and the blues and minstrel culture before that.

A major tension for Black Twitter users and for Black digital culture overall is the same that marks African-American life in general: the problem of living in spaces not designed for you even though they are built and operate in relation to professed egalitarian ideals. For example, Twitter co-founder and CEO Jack Dorsey seemed to endorse Black activism and the power of #BlackTwitter by wearing a t-shirt emblazoned with the #StayWoke hashtag and Twitter bird logo at the 2016 Code Conference while the site itself continued to face challenges protecting vulnerable users from racist, sexist, and homophobic attacks. At the conference, Dorsey participated in a conversation with Peter Kafka, senior editor of *Media*, and DeRay McKesson, who, along with Johnetta Elzie and Brittany Packayetti, were active in the Ferguson protests and founders of Campaign Zero, an effort to advocate for justice generally and to end police violence specifically in and beyond Ferguson. McKesson raised the safety concerns regarding Twitter, and Kafka subsequently asked, "Does a platform *have* to be neutral?" Dorsey's reply was, "I think a platform is best when it carries every voice." ("What Is Twitter," youtube.com). This prompted Jia Tolentino (2017) to accuse Dorsey, the head of a company with a 3 percent Black and Latino workforce, of "comfy, self-serving, and distracting political stagnation of performative allyship." Similarly, Twitter user @nyashajunior charged inconsistency on Dorsey's part. While posting the link to Tolentino's write up, she highlighted the following words: "you can't #staywoke and then call yourself neutral" (https://twitter.com/NyashaJunior/status/739269185134415873).

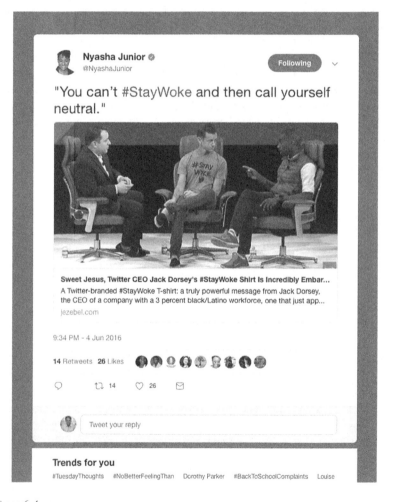

Figure 6.4

In many ways, #BlackTwitter *is* Twitter. The power of Black Twitter from the everyday and playful and participatory to the critical and resistant brought new life to the service when some analysts had spent years predicting its demise. #BlackLivesMatter era protests initiated, led, and sustained by Black women, and especially the protests, actions, and conversations related to Ferguson after the killing of Michael Brown, gave Twitter an importance beyond just random tweets about monotonous day-to-day activities and other ephemera. This sense of the site's value as a social or even public good was meant to be symbolized by the joint appearance of Dorsey and McKesson. But even as Dorsey's choice of the #StayWoke t-shirt branded with Twitter's logo and his comments affirmed this connection, his remarks focused on the importance of the site rather than on the importance of the distinct ways that people have used and even transformed it.

The gendered nature of Black erasure should never be minimized. Just as #BlackTwitter drives Twitter, Black women drive #BlackTwitter, often without significant credit. One example within-community erasure emerged during the height of Ferguson and Black Lives Matter protests. In their study *Beyond the Hashtags: #Ferguson, #BlackLivesMatter and the Online Struggle for Offline Justice*," Deen Freelon, Charlton McIlWain, and Meredith Clark (2016) note while the Twitter discussions of police violence, structural inequalities, and activism against these injustices was Black-led, male voices were often the most amplified despite the fact that Black women led much of the activism nationwide and the discussion on Twitter:

> Scanning the ranks of each period's top five user lists, it is plain to see that men are overrepresented. While women appear regularly among each period's hubs, only one of the 10 most-referenced users is a woman (Johnetta Elzie/@nettaaaaaaaa). It seems unlikely that this distribution of retweets and mentions rewards women's contributions proportionally . . . . The choice to lift up the voices of certain individuals over others is not a neutral one, though its political implications may not be perceived by those who make it. Retweets and replies may not always be endorsements, but they do partially determine which participants are seen as experts and leaders. Put more directly, they confer power, and the women in our dataset have not received a proportionate share.
>
> (p. 76)

The authors describe the complexities of the problem as resting between the openness of Internet culture, in which influencers cannot control the popularity of hashtags or other kinds of content once they start to spread, and the multiple media venues that still privilege some voices over others according to entrenched patterns of power and exclusion (p. 83). To put it another way, while #BlackTwitter is indeed a "cultural conversation," as Andre Brock rightly called it (2012, p. 530), it is also still a public one and subject to the same racism, sexism, and homophobia that bear so heavily on all aspects of American life, online and off—even within activist efforts working to dismantle these inequalities and the forms of violence that are endemic to them.

When Signifyin + Call-and-Response = Nommo

There are times when the instances of signifyin and call-and-response that are so central to how #BlackTwitter works rhetorically combine to become something far more powerful than the sum of the individual participants or their tweets. They emerge into Nommo, defined as the belief in the pervasive, mystical, transformative, even life-giving power of the Word (Smitherman, 1977, p. 78). One way to understand Nommo at work in Black rhetoric is when something transformative happens through people, language, occasion, and timing coming together. The sermon becomes more than a sermon. Janelle Monáe and the Wondaland Artist Collective's "Hell You Talmbout" (2015) and Kendrick Lamar's "Alright" (2015) became anthems resisting sexism, racism, and police violence. #BlackLivesMatter, #SayHerName, and #YouOKSis became lasting concepts far more powerful than simply the collectives of Twitter users and tweets that referenced, shared, or commented on them.

Another of these moments began to unfold in fall 2016. On November 13, 2016, Instagram user @iComplexity uploaded a video mash-up using a remix of Shirley Caesar's classic song "Hold My Mule" created by Suede the Remix God. Not only was a new viral meme created, but an intergenerational Nommo event transpired as well. The remix and the videos that exploded in response to a "You Name It Challenge" was based on the looping of a line from the song—"Look! I got greens, beans, potatoes, tomatoes . . . you name it!"—over a hip-hop beat. Part of the popularity of the remix and the associated "challenge" to create other videos and content related to the meme comes from the fact that it was released near the Thanksgiving holiday. And just as the holiday is a time when families come together offline, it is also a time when a #BlackTwitter family reunion happens, with ongoing conversations that become trending topics on all kinds of subjects from the serious to the silly.

"Hold My Mule," was released in 1988 and re-released in 2011. It tells the story of a character named Shoutin John. The song and story serve as a cautionary tale to those who, because of middle-class success, have gotten too fancy and have abandoned less dignified (read: vernacular) practices like shouting, dancing, and speaking in tongues during worship. In the story, a group of deacons from a small church drive their fancy cars and go to visit Shoutin John because members of their small church have grown tired of his effusive praise, even threatening to kick him out of the church if he does not change. When confronted with their complaint, Shoutin John stops working on his farmland to tell the deacons exactly why he shouts, why his praise is so enthusiastic. It is because all of the considerable size of his property and the fact that all of the food that comes from that land, from his work, is his—as opposed to the fancy cars for which the deacons are presumably still paying. "Hold my mule" has long been a saying meant as a warning: in the sacred tradition, a warning that someone is about to be overcome with praise; on the secular side, a warning that there might be a confrontation. The song "Hold My Mule" is delivered by Caesar as a warning and a class critique that black folk should not get so content with "success" that they stray from, in the Gospel rendering, the God that brought them there, or, in the broader sense, from the practices that got them over through difficult times to success.

The loop from the song became an unofficial beginning to the reunion. Shirley Caesar's delivery and the intense gaze of one of the choir members as Caesar announces "Look!" became occasions to celebrate Black expressive culture generally, and vernacular Black expression specifically. The looping of a hip-hop beat, heavy on drum and bass, over a recognized gospel song by a beloved gospel singer and pastor became a compelling rendering of the Saturday-night-and-Sunday-morning continuum in Black culture and exemplified the fact that there is no easy separation between spiritual and secular, between sacred and profane.

The video by iComplexity takes all of these elements and distills them through instantly recognizable moments in Black performance from music to television. Dance moves by people in their own cars to the Aunt Viv character in *Fresh Prince of Bel Air*, to Gina and Martin from the sitcom *Martin*, to Prince himself are all edited so their dances fit perfectly with the beats and loop from Caesar. The freedom in the dance moves extends the merging of different points along the sacred and secular continuum, celebrating the bold, the irreverent, even what in this contemporary moment would be referred to as ratchet. Queer Black culture is celebrated in the dance moves selected for the video every bit as much as popular "mainstream" figures and television shows like *Martin* and *Fresh Prince of Bel Air*.

#YouNameIt became more than a meme, however, more than a trending topic on Twitter and other sites, and more than an index of viral content. The combination of signifyin and call-and-response that is crucial to Black rhetoric and Black digital culture came together to create a larger phenomenon. Untold legions of people from unknown users to celebrities with millions of followers created their own #YouNameIt remixes, and the challenge brought Shirley Caesar herself back into celebrity, as she first celebrated the meme and those who circulated the remix videos and then later expressed concerns about intellectual property and credit.

The #YouNameIt meme, the references to "greens, beans, potatoes, tomatoes" and to "Hold My Mule," all combine to demonstrate the central place vernacular expression plays in Black digital culture, across class, education, and location. They also show the power of remix culture to do what Tricia Rose called for more than twenty years ago in *Black Noise*: "imagine these Hip Hop principles as a blueprint for social resistance and affirmation: create sustaining narratives, accumulate them, layer, embellish, and transform them" (1994, p. 39). This one-minute video built off of a remix built off of a loop from a classic gospel song brings together not only hip hop and gospel, secular and sacred. It also signifies Black access to mainstream media and celebrates voices that have been relegated to the margins. It highlights polished and vernacular, oral tradition and visual culture, digital and analog, "old school" and futuristic.

In summary, the significance of the rhetorical practices that make #Black-Twitter such a vibrant space for Black public, counterpublic, and underground discourse lies not only in the fact that interactions among its participants have led to real, offline impact through activism, community building, advocacy, love, professional success, and more. Examining Twitter through a technocultural lens, Brock (2012) stated, "it becomes remarkable that Black discourse can be employed effectively over a medium designed for a small, technologically proficient, mostly White user base" (p. 534). To put it differently, Black technology users, bringing Black discourse and ways of seeing the world, transformed Twitter.

#BlackTwitter as a phenomenon is also a reminder that the obstacles that have always been a part of African-American life offline are built into the technologies we use to interact online as well. Scholar and cultural critic Mark Anthony Neal highlights this changing same in a post on his digital platform NewBlackMan (in Exile), "'If You Don't Own the [Servers]': Curating + Aggregating + Doing Black Digital Studies in the Digital Era." In this reflection on Black digital studies, Neal looks back at the launch of H-AfroAm, a listserv and Black digital studies project launched by Abdul Alkalimat, and places it in much-needed perspective. It was of critical importance for Alkalimat that he owned the servers that held the content and conversations of Black scholars connected to the intellectual project of Black Studies. This need remains, even as Black people participate on wide-ranging popular platforms like Twitter, because, as Neal points out, "the servers that power Facebook, Twitter, Instagram, Snapchat and process the massive data of those operations are not owned by those who share interests in Black Liberation projects, even as the narratives of Black liberation provide needed content for these platforms." Paraphrasing sentiments expressed by Professor Marisa Parham at a recent gathering at Johns Hopkins University, Neal writes, "#BlackTwitter is an apt metaphor for the exploitation of Black Digital innovation; #BlackTwitter helped Twitter figure out what its own power was."

Black joy, play, activism, liberation work, resistance, and other responses to abuse, structural inequality, and targeted violence all converge in Black rhetorical traditions and practices to such a degree that all of these and more might be present in any one moment, text, image, video, or performance, network, archive, or connection. The story of #BlackTwitter as a case study in African-American rhetoric is a story of this confluence and the practices that make it possible. It is also the story of Black innovation in digital culture in a time of technological convergence.

Notes

1. Rhetorician Vorris Nunley, in *Keepin' It Hushed* (2011), has developed the notion of African-American hush harbor rhetoric (AAHHR). He has been concerned with "bringing into theoretical purview and scholarly consideration a continually evolving tradition of risky speech, hidden transcripts, and productive subjugated

knowledges by and for African Americans" p. 23. He explained his nomenclature this way: "I borrow the term *hush harbor* from enslaved Africans and African Americans. They used the term and others such as *hush arbor* and *bush arbor* to refer to geographies such as the slave quarters, woods, and praise houses where Black folks could speak frankly in Black spaces in front of Black audiences. In these hush harbor spaces, Black rhetors and speakers were free to engage in and deploy otherwise heavily monitored practices, knowledges, and rhetorics disallowed in the public sphere under the disciplining gaze of Whites and Whiteness. In informal, unofficial meeting places such as cane breaks, woods, praise houses, funeral parlors, jook joints, the Chitlin' Circuit, and their contemporary manifestations in beauty shops and barbershops, hush harbor geographies were/are quasi-public or hidden spaces where Blackness on parallel, alternative, and lower frequencies circulates," pp. 23–4.

2. The term *Jes Grew* stems from Harriet Beecher Stowe's *Uncle Tom's Cabin*. In the novel, Miss Ophelia asks Topsy, a young and enslaved girl, if she knew who made her. Topsy replies, "Nobody, as I knows on . . . . I spect I grow'd. Don't think nobody never made me," (p. 356). James Weldon Johnson likely heard the particular phrasing "jes grew" in a stage production, and he subsequently used it as a simile in his preface to *The Book of American Negro Poetry* to describe the origin of ragtime songs, writing, "The earliest Ragtime songs, like Topsy, "jes' grew"" (p. 12). Picking up on Johnson's usage, Ishmael Reed used the moniker Jes Grew to personify ragtme, jazz, and a general sense of freedom in his 1972 novel, *Mumbo Jumbo*.

3. "The politics of respectability" describes the attempt by members of marginalized groups to align the mores of those groups with the so-called respectable mainstream. Moreover, it is the deployment of that ideal to chastise or critique in-group behavior. The phrase has become popular since Evelyn Brooks Higginbotham's (1993) historical study, *Righteous Discontent: The Women's Movement in the Black Baptist Church, 1880–1920*.

4. See Quintilian (2015), *Institutes of Oratory*, pp. 3, 96, 101.

5. The #Zola story was posted by user @_zolarmoon October 27, 2015 and instantly became an Internet sensation, generating not only legions of tweets in response, but media reports by *Time*, CNN, the *Washington Post*, the *Daily Mail*, and other news outlets. A Twitter search of "regional slander" or "NY slander" will show examples of these roast sessions, but podcasters Desus Nice and The Kid Mero, now hosts of a late-night television show on the Vice network, popularized these roasts beyond Twitter on their podcast "The Bodega Boys."

6. Fanon's use of the phrase "night and day surveillance" is recorded in Peter Geismar's *Fanon*, (1971, p. 185).

7 College-Writing Instruction and African-American Rhetoric

The labels Rhet/Comp and Comp/Rhet, which are common designators in American colleges and universities, represent the fusion of rhetoric studies and composition studies. African-American scholars and practitioners have long had a major presence in and influence on the field. They have sometimes been proponents of a prescriptive, analytic paradigm in which the focus is on finished texts and textual features with little regard for the circumstances of their creation and against an inflexible standard of correctness. Termed the product approach, this mode of instruction dominated the composition landscape for several generations, and it was predictable that, because ruling education constructs prove to be cogent across various segments of the professoriate, many African-American instructors adhered to it. Dialect was seen as deficit, and the message to students was that they must get standardized right away or get out. Many students failed writing courses—and college—on that basis. On the other hand, African Americans have valiantly contributed to the development of alternate conceptions of composition teaching, approaches that consider, as Clark and Ivanič (1997) outlined, politics, purpose, and process, as well as product (p. 17). This more progressive and enabling pedagogy values African-American language practices and is the superior approach to producing large numbers of educated, critical, and astute African-American students. It is the tradition with which we are presently concerned.

Important forerunners in this latter movement include elocutionist, activist, and educator Hallie Quinn Brown (1880, 1910, 1975) and historian Carter G. Woodson. Brown, the most notable African-American college language educator at the beginning of the twentieth century, included material written in African-American Vernacular English in her reciter text *Bits and Odds* (1880). She exhibited such cultural and linguistic sensitivity throughout her lengthy career, which included the teaching of numerous sections of Freshman English. Woodson agreed with Brown's basic technique. In *The Mis-education of the Negro* (1933/1990), he observed,

> In the study of language in school pupils were made to scoff at the Negro dialect as some peculiar possession of the Negro which they should

despise rather than directed to study the background of this language as a broken-down African tongue—in short to understand their own linguistic history.

(p. 19)

He argued furthermore that African-American students should be exposed in school to African folklore and proverbs as well as to the works of African-American writers (p. 150).

Following Brown and Woodson, who passed away within months of each other at mid-century, African-American practitioners and scholars pushed further on the issue of relevant pedagogy. For instance, Juanita Williamson (1957) published "What Can We Do About It?—The Contribution of Linguistics to the Teaching of English" in *CLA Journal*, the organ of the Black-founded and Black-run College Language Association (CLA), which was the main organization where African Americans debated writing pedagogy. Williamson addressed the inadequacy of popular and prescriptive handbooks. Instead of favoring skill-and-drill techniques, she understood that student motivation—another way of saying politics and purpose—is a crucial factor in education. Asserting the worth of contrastive language analysis, she wrote with regard to the students she taught, "If we show him the structure of standard English and the structure of his own dialect, he will see what change he should make, and *if he wishes*, he will do so" (pp. 26–7, emphasis added). Of course, instructors could play a role in shaping students' dispositions, and never is there only one way to do so.

At the 1958 CLA Annual Convention, Nettie Parler of South Carolina State College described a detailed program for teaching African-American students. In response to the sharply rising enrollments of students from working-class backgrounds, her institution had replaced traditional English courses with communications courses and established the Communications Center, which offered remediation in addition to college composition courses. The center had a decidedly eradicationist mission, as Parler described:

I do recognize nevertheless that incorrect language habits are amoebic in nature. They grow prolifically and vigorously on our college campuses, and they are most difficult to control. Although a strong, determined drive against them should be spearheaded by the English staff of each college, control can only be accomplished through the vigilance and efforts of the entire faculty, with each instructor unequivocally demanding that the students of his classes speak, listen, read and write correctly at all times. In this manner not only shall we dissipate the widely accepted rumor that good English need merely be written and spoken in the English class, for the English teacher; but we shall raise the level of our students in the communications areas to an inestimable height.

(p. 50)

Immediately following, however, Parler urged a more nurturing, developmental approach:

> I, therefore, exhort all who teach to follow the golden rule of education which states that we must begin with the learner where he is. That is the only way to educate. Any effort to superimpose upon the learner subject manner for which he is not prepared is a waste of time and energy for both the student and the teacher.
>
> (p. 50)

She demonstrated in one good-hearted but conflicted presentation the major terms of the debate about composition instruction among African-American educators and others as well.

By the late 1960s, much of the scholarly deliberation had shifted to the Conference on College Composition and Communication (CCCC). CCCC was sort of the desegregating White university analog alongside the HBCU (Historically Black Colleges and Universities) role of CLA. Several CLA members joined the younger organization while retaining membership in the former. In the pages of *College Composition and Communication*, Ernece Kelly (1968) spoke out against racist curricular practices and against racism throughout the profession. Along with noting the virtual exclusion of Black participants from the 1968 CCCC annual convention, she expressed dismay over "the awful resistance of white participants to the challenges to recognize their biases and to work to defeat them" (p. 107). Several issues later, Marian Musgrave (1971) expounded on class, caste, and racial bias in American colleges and universities. In one of the earliest essays to consider jointly Black and non-Black colleges, Musgrave argued that many Freshman Composition courses were disabling for students. Recognizing that American education historically reproduced inequity, she scolded teachers for ignoring the findings of linguistics and challenged the assertion that Black English was damaging to African-American students. She proposed that composition teachers resist their tendencies to reject African-American Vernacular English and the students who speak it: "Black teachers have had to slough off their old attitudes quickly under the new black militancy, whereas whites have often hurried to find a new rationale for their old evil. I assure you that sloughing is better" (p. 29).

Meanwhile, in CLA, Jessie Brown (1968), who would head the Black Caucus inside CCCC, advanced a complementary argument and stressed a personal-growth model for Black students that, unlike the prescriptive aspects of Parler's proposal, would emphasize the resources of their native language varieties. In "Advanced Composition," Brown spoke of students increasing their language power as a means of extending their selves, the necessity of focusing on student writing as the primary texts of instruction, and the efficacy of constructive teacher and peer criticism. The essay emphasized, too, that composition students should experiment with various nonfiction genres and purposes, and that the field of composition should embrace insights made available by literary analysis, generative grammar, rhetoric, and logic. Brown's article can be seen as an African-American equivalent of, or even response to, the famous Dartmouth Seminar held in 1966,[1] though Brown was predictably critical of the lack of African-American participation at that event. Also in *CLA*, Melvin Butler (1971) of Southern University addressed the subject of Black dialect and teaching English relative to HBCUS, and, like Musgrave, he lambasted African Americans who denied their own heritage for the sake of culturally dominant formulations. As he wrote,

> any English program that claims as its model Harvard, Yale, or Princeton but enrolls as its students sons and daughters, sisters and brothers, babies and knee babies, friends and lovers of Harvard's, Yale's, and Princeton's janitors is a program with a built-in margin for failure that staggers the mind.
>
> (p. 239)

In November 1971, Butler was named by the CCCC Executive Committee to head a group that would compose a position statement on students' dialects.[2] A year later, the Committee adopted the resultant resolution:

> We affirm the students' right to their own language—the dialects of their nurture or whatever dialects in which they find their own identity and style. Language scholars long ago denied that the myth of a standard American dialect has any validity. The claim that any one dialect is unacceptable amounts to an attempt of one social group to exert its dominance over another. Such a claim leads to false advice for speakers and writers, and immoral advice for humans. A nation proud of its diverse heritage and its cultural and racial variety will preserve its heritage of dialects. We affirm strongly that teachers must have the experiences and training that will enable them to respect diversity and uphold the right of students to their own language.
>
> (Corbett, 1974)

CCCC membership eventually accepted the measure in 1974, and the organization devoted a special issue of *College Composition and Communication* both to disseminate the resolution and to provide elaboration about the document's premises and implications.

"Students' Right" remains controversial. How is such right to be granted in colleges and universities? How is writing in "their own language" to be evaluated? These questions continue to be discussed, and various proposals have been proffered. For example, in 1985 the Black Caucus published *Tapping Potential*, the first major all-Black book in language arts and composition. Not only a response to "Students' Right," the book is in some ways a tribute to Carter G. Woodson; his thoughts about language and literature as well as his focus on African-American identity and self-knowledge resonate prominently in lead editor Charlotte Brooks's foreword and throughout the collection. Delores Lipscomb edited the section on writing, which includes entries such as Janis Epps's "Killing Them Softly: Why Willie Can't Write," Jacqueline Royster's "A New Lease on Writing," Paul Ramsey's "Teaching the Teachers to Teach Black-Dialect Writers," Vivian Davis's "Teachers as Editors: The Student Conference," and Edward Anderson's "Using Folk Literature in Teaching Composition."

The most certain long-term result of "Students' Right" is that serious composition teaching and scholarship reflect a favorable view of language variety. Such diversity is considered an opportunity and not simply an obstacle, challenge, or reason to disqualify students or recycle them through suspect remediation programs. This line of reasoning has been consistently articulated by linguist and rhetorician Geneva Smitherman, who served on the committee that produced "Students' Right" and emerged as the central African-American figure in composition studies. In *Talkin and Testifyin: The Language of Black America* (1977), she explained:

> Communicative competence, quite simply, refers to the ability to communicate effectively. At this point, however, all simplicity ends. For to be able to speak or write with power is a very complex business, involving a universe of linguistic choices and alternatives. Such a speaker or writer must use language that is appropriate to the situation and the audience. He or she must be able to answer such questions as: who can say what to whom, under what conditions? who is my audience? what assumptions can I make about that audience? What are its interests, concerns, range of knowledge? in a given act of speaking or writing, what examples or details will fit best and where? I am here talking about aspects of communication such as content and message, style, choice of words, logical development, analysis and arrangement, originality of thought and expression, and so forth. Such are the real components of language power, and they cannot be measured or mastered by narrow conceptions of "correct grammar." While teachers frequently correct student language on the basis of such misguided conceptions, saying something correctly, and saying it well, are two entirely different Thangs.
>
> (pp. 228–9)

By commenting expansively about rhetoric and championing the rigorous pursuit of rhetorical power over slavish adherence to "correct grammar," she tried to ward off the criticism that embracing linguistic diversity necessarily entails a relaxing of worthwhile standards.

Smitherman reaffirmed her approach to writing instruction in an essay titled "Toward Educational Linguistics for the First World" (1979):

> Writing instruction should be geared toward the recognition of audience, context, and situation, and students should be given opportunities to

experiment with the various kinds of communication in their linguistic bags. Reports and memos are not the same as directions for workers, which are not the same as letters to friends. Development of communicative competence requires knowledge of the efficacy of different registers and forms in different contexts and an understanding of how language works in its natural social settings.

(p. 210)

In 1994, Smitherman published the results of a significant study, "The Blacker the Berry, the Sweeter the Juice," which demonstrated a positive correlation between African-American discourse patterns and high marks received on a large sample of student essays examined as part of the National Assessment of Educational Progress (NAEP) (p. 93). She concluded that, "regardless of rhetorical modality," the expressive qualities of the African-American verbal tradition enable students, granted ample rewriting and revision, to produce essays that are "lively," "image-filled," "concrete," and "readable" (p. 95).

Elaine Richardson (2003), Smitherman's student and protégé, vigorously responds to her mentor's work. In *African American Literacies*, she reflects on her affecting sociolinguistic journey, which has included her roles as a college composition student, language theorist, cultural critic, and education researcher, and she describes how that journey has fueled her scholarship. As a student, because of a prose style closely reflective of her upbringing, surroundings, and experiences in 1960s and 1970s urban Cleveland, she encountered more difficulty with writing teachers and tutors than with completing writing assignments. Eventually, she figured out that she could succeed in class, which to her came to mean the unenthusiastic reception of a "C," if, in that context, she submitted to "Whitenization" and relinquished her "language variety, history, experience, culture, and perspective" (p. 2). "Ah, the price for a 'C' was high," she ruefully reminisces, "the subordination of my experience and the erasure of my voice paralleling the absence of Black voices and culturally relevant material and instruction in the curriculum and the classroom" (p. 2). Richardson knew that she was not alone but shared a situation, if not necessarily outcome, with numerous African-American students. As an academic, she has proposed a solution to alienation that was not available to her in her circumstance: an African American-centered writing curriculum.

Rejecting the idea that language could ever be taught in colleges legitimately without faculty and students consciously considering power and politics, Richardson wants the substance of what she terms White-supremacist and capitalist-based literacy instruction made plain—its emphasis on detachment, objectivity, positivism, conformity, and a mythic meritocracy (p. 9). These are pretty unappealing options in the Black rhetorical tradition, and, in fact, Richardson blames White-supremacist, capitalist approaches for much of Black literacy underachievement. Thus, her countering pedagogical move, African American-centered composition theory, is based on four assumptions:

1. Form and content are inextricably bound
2. Black Discourse is an Academic Discourse in constant flux, in negotiation with other discourse, including the dominant discourse
3. Contrastive analysis of AAVE syntax and discourse against standardized syntax and discourse will result in students' improved critical language facilities
4. Increased historical and cultural self consciousness and critical awareness can be realized in writing and discourse showing Black discourse features.

(p. 97)

Although all four premises are important, Richardson perhaps considers the first, the form-content link, or the field dependency presented as a Black discourse style by Smitherman in her NAEP study, to be the most intriguing. Field dependency is defined as "involvement with and immersion in events and situations; personalizing phenomenon; lack of distance from topics and subjects" (Richardson, p. 156), and Richardson reflects, "I would argue that field dependency is the hallmark of the Black style, a signature feature . . . [it] epitomizes the person-centered assumptions of AAVE culture. It helps a writer to engage more deeply with the subject" (pp. 109–10). Responding once again to the vexing milieu in which she once participated as an undergraduate, she concludes, "Generally, field dependency is in opposition to traditionally conceived 'objectivity' and 'neutrality' that characterizes academic discourse" (p. 110).

As to the specifics of her research, Richardson collected data from fifty-two students whom she taught in several sections of her African-American-centered course at a Big Ten university. Driven by the query "is writing enhanced by African American methodology?" (p. 100), she had students read a background statement about language, racism, and the experiences of writers of African descent (p. 100) and then respond, as a pre-test, to a prompt: "What does it mean to be Black and write or to be Black and literate?" (p. 101). The students were not asked to try to produce Black discourse styles, but they were invited the do so if they wished. They were only required to give the assignment their best shot. Using several statistical measurements, Richardson found no significant correlation between test scores and AAVE syntax features like *zero copula* (the movie good), *habitual be* (she be in the gym), or *ed morpheme* (he look for it already). However, there was a significant negative correlation between essay length and AAVE syntax: the longer the paper, the less frequent appearance of AAVE syntax (p. 103). There was a significant negative correlation between AAVE syntax and Black discourse features: the more discourse features, the less AAVE syntax (p. 103). Therefore, her findings matched those of Smitherman and suggested that when students were encouraged to tap into all of their linguistic resources without worrying about being detached-objective-good-English-perfect, or without fear of "error" or penalty, they flow better, produce less "error," and perhaps encounter less penalty. In any event, AAVE usage was not an impediment to student writing (p. 105). Most important, in her analysis of post-test results, a barometer of her actual teaching, Richardson saw better performances and additional positive correlations among Black discourse, essay length, and rater scores (p. 105). She had brand-new empirical justification for her curriculum.

Near the end of her discussion of this phase of her research, Richardson opines, "I think by integrating the speech styles, rhetorical, and literacy traditions of African Americans into academic writing, we invite students to have a fair fight with discourse" (p. 113). And at the close of her book, she writes, "Black discourse and rhetoric helped to evolve and revolutionize the meaning of equality in this country. We cannot afford to continue to subjugate this discourse in the classroom" (p. 149). She means, of course, that we must squarely confront the history and politics of literacy, recognize the arbitrary nature of language standards, and refuse to use Black language as a reason to fail Black students.

Closely aligned with Richardson's scholarship, Kermit Campbell (2005), in *Gettin' Our Groove On*, speaks to and illustrates the value to African-American students and perhaps to all students of rap or, more precisely, of "writing imbued with rap sensibilities" (p. 133). He has encouraged students to produce such writing because he finds that its analytic power, its literate representation, and inspection of personal, cultural, and political tensions, are crucial to the further development of critical perspectives and preferable to a string of expository assignments that privilege the illusions of authorial distance and objectivity. This does not mean that he totally wants to displace thesis-driven academic writing. His book, though hip-hop inflected, is primarily of that type. Thus, he acknowledges,

> Of course, students should learn how to write, say, effective arguments (the mantra at my old, old job), but our personal lives are in fact arguments, are embedded in argument. And besides, an argument is so much more meaningful when the writer's personal knowledge and experience, her subjectivity, suffuse it.
>
> (p. 140)

Campbell wants students to speak back to the academy and help push it toward greater equity and vitality rather to settle only for the stamp of the status quo. He only hints at a critique of White hegemony (p. 143), but he is clear that promotion of rap-imbued writing and its engagement with texts and ideologies of the so-called mainstream potentially improve discourse for all. In other words, the curriculum he advocates produces new student insights that we would do well to consider. Drawing inspiration from Mary Louise Pratt and her influential essay, "Arts of the Contact Zone," Campbell conceives of classrooms in which activities flourish relative to, following Pratt's recommendations, storytelling, the forging of identifications, the consideration of vernacular forms, and the redemption of the oral. Rap is a ready medium for all of that activity and is, in Campbell's view, an integral aspect of the verbal repertoires of many African-American students as they experiment with options for producing rhetorically powerful texts.[3]

Vershawn Young (2007) agrees with Campbell's approach and, like Campbell, he provides, in *Your Average Nigga*, a masterfully written, poly-vocal book that models the writing that we could be helping students produce. Working out of a framework that he terms the "sociolinguistics of racial performance" (p. 3), Young advocates the promotion of code meshing as the best pedagogical strategy in writing classrooms. He affirms the critique that schools largely have functioned to reproduce the status quo, allowing sporadic individual mobility but not yet facilitating much group elevation. Of course, like several of his intellectual predecessors, Young understands that a key aspect of social management has been to designate language varieties such as AAVE to be illegitimate vehicles for expression and instruction in schools. That teachers accede to such demarcation is, in Young's account, the explanation for many of the struggles and much of the so-called failure experienced by African-American students in first-year writing courses. Even as language researchers establish an unequivocal case for linguistic equality, teachers and administrators, unable to refute research logically, often offer code-switching pedagogy as a concession to it: Use code switching as a way to bridge, say, AAVE and Standardized American English, but make sure assessments are only of written performance in the standardized language variety. Rejecting that dictate, Young argues,

> True linguistic and identity integration would mean allowing students to do what I call code meshing based on what linguists have called code mixing, to combine dialects, styles, and registers. This technique meshes versions of English together in a way that's more in line with how people actually speak and write anyway.
>
> (p. 7)

Although "code meshing" is an admirable addition to the field's critical vocabulary, it is not necessarily the opposite of code switching in strictly linguistic terms. We make this comment to lower the temperature of some of the contemporary mesh vs. switch debates. After all, language, for all practical purposes, is a monophonic instrument; we can only say one word at a time. Whether an ensuing word, say functioning as part of a standardized construction, is part of a mesh pattern or switch pattern can only be determined by extending the utterance. What length or timeframe regarding utterances determines whether we are meshing or switching? The answer can become very detailed and take us far afield. Our point is that we should focus on practice rather than debates about terminology, especially when the debaters share pretty much the same pedagogical orientation. Therefore, the value of Young's coinage lies not in the linguistic distinction it tries to make but in the unmistakable clarity it brings to purported progressive expectations set by teachers. If they are not inviting students, particularly, for Young's purposes, poor African-American students, to submit papers that feature the range of their linguistic versatility, then they are cooperating in a systemic project of political suppression and disqualification no matter how they explain their cur-riculums. Moreover, Young knows that experimenting with hybrid discourses could make for better writing (p. 121). You have to master several language varieties to be a master of the written mesh.

Although he details no overarching political vision, Young remains an invigorating voice in composition studies and clear in his critique. Opposing a narrow utilitarian or marketplace imperative, he declares, "We should prepare students for societal change, not merely to fit in" (p. 112). He does not mention the other N word, neoliberalism, as does Vorris Nunley (2011), who argues that "neoliberalism as a political rationality functions as pedagogy that normalizes a constellation of values around market logics" and alongside that observation contends, "my personal goal in the composition classroom is to develop more effective writers, critical thinkers, critical citizens, more competent users of literacies, and fewer citizen subjects as *Homo econimicus*" (p. 158). Yet Young believes, as he remains sympathetic to the plight of students, "we should stop hating on the playas and start assessing the whole game" (p. 145).

Absorbing various lessons of the Black Freedom Struggle, Carmen Kynard, in *Vernacular Insurrections* (2013), performs the most explicitly Black-radical intervention in composition studies. She does so in two ways. First, through a stellar project of revisionist historiography, she extends the boundaries of origins discourse about modern composition studies, or since the beginning of the "Students Right" era, by arguing compellingly that protesting students and intellectuals were the primary agents who brought modern composition studies into existence. They were not tangential to the field in the 1960s, and, in fact, Black student activists and radical intellectuals from the 1920s onward, particularly those connected to Historically Black Colleges and Universities (HBCUS), never had been. Kynard thus posits the Black Freedom Struggle and its imperative to democratize higher education overall as necessary precondi-tions to the creation of the composition programs we now see at predominately White institutions. Kynard's narrative counters a story of liberal uplift efforts by well-meaning White faculty. To be clear, Kynard does not contend that well-meaning White faculty members were unimportant. She simply wants the historical record to show that well-meaning activist students of color were the most important factor in the development of writing pedagogy responsive to their needs.

Kynard's second challenge to composition studies orthodoxy is pedagogical. In her view, anyone who is teaching from a conception that does not incor-porate the Black Freedom Struggle is doing students a disservice because such teaching does not encourage the most insightful view of the contemporary world. Kynard's teaching mission is one of "activist rhetorical education" (p. 7). She privileges deep investigations of reading of texts, pushing for clarity about how texts function in relation to political networks. This is akin to what some know as critical pedagogy and the goal of having students become critical language consumers and producers. But what distinguishes Kynard is her bold embrace of Black radicalism, partly expressed in five "breakdowns" or expressed consolidations of her desire to promote anticapitalist, antiracist teaching and research that specifically address the lives of working-class African Americans:

1. Can you get down with some good ole-fashioned political economy rather than just peppering the words *capitalism* and *class* here and there? Can you locate class as superstructure rather than merely an "identity" that enables the ignoring of whiteness?
2. Are you trying to get everyone to move on up like the Jeffersons or can you critique the displacement and exploitation that them "deluxe apartments in the sky-high" create?
3. Are you forever and a day talking about using the master's tools to get into his house, or are you trying to move to new land?
4. Do you talk about black folk as objects of study without ever sitting at the table with them, living beside them?
5. Are you doing something other than writing books and articles, going to conferences? Who and where you be on and off the academic plantation?

For Kynard, progressive responses to these questions reflect the best aspects of the legacy of "The Students' Right to Their Own Language"—and of Smitherman, one of her sources of inspiration (pp. 100–1).

Although we know her political disposition, Kynard is not domineering in classrooms. In the "teaching interludes" that she presents, we detect no dogmatism. It is not specific syllabi or assignments that matter much. But essential to Kynard is some, however flexible, engagement with ideas about structural racism, U.S. education history, the long Civil Rights Movement, Black Power, the rise of Black Studies, the role of HBCUS, vernacular cultures, the Black Arts Movement, and sociolinguistic knowledge of African-American Language, among others. "All that ain't a lesson plan," she declares; "it is a political disposition that shapes what and why you do what you do in the classroom." Paraphrasing Zora Neale Hurston relative to the value of broad experience, she advises, "*You gotta go there to teach there.*[4] The light at the end of the tunnel is this: we have precedents, examples, and inspiration if we clear out what has gotten in the way" (pp. 247–8).

One of the precedents that Kynard acknowledges is subsequently explored in detail by Rhea Lathan (2015) in *Freedom Writing*, as she examines the history of the South Carolina Sea Islands Citizenship Schools (later dubbed Freedom Schools), which were established as a modest entity in 1955 by Septima Clark, Myles Horton, Esau Jenkins, Bernice Robinson, and others. Citizenship schools eventually were formed throughout the South and involved more than 60,000 participants (p. iii), who understood for the most part that literacy was essential to constructing the lives they desired to live. This was clearly a political understanding. They grasped the idea that who was encouraged to write and who was doomed *not* to write was a product of power relations, and they knew that for African Americans to claim literacy during the era of Jim Crow represented a radical act. Although voter registration obviously became a focus of the schools, the literacy vision was broader. An excerpt from an instructional manual, My *Citizenship Booklet*, reads, "But there is involved in the mechanics of learning to read and write an all-around education in community development which includes housing, recreation, health and improved home life" (quoted in Lathan, p. 77).

To deepen her comprehension of the citizenship-schools phenomenon, Lathan employs an epistemological frame that she labels "gospel literacy" (p. xvii), a concept that follows from her observation that many civil-rights activities occurred in churches and prayer meetings and that gospel consciousness (sacred) and the literacy outpouring of the Freedom movement (secular) evolved together, influencing one another within a Black cultural formation that animated both (p. xvii).

Gospel literacy contains four dominant precepts:

1. acknowledging the burden
2. call-and-response
3. bearing witness
4. finding redemption.

(p. xvii)

Lathan illustrates each idea by referring to the everyday actions of participants in civic contexts. For example, to accept the burden was to honor the sacrifice of courageous forbears and rise to the challenge of transforming society for the better.

Call-and-response was evident in the back-and-forth flow between pupils/ organizers and instructors/administrators/organizers as they continually modified curricula and political agendas in response to personal needs, differing on various occasions and on some initiatives but remaining united organically in a liberating struggle (pp. 66–72). Bearing witness, the expectation that provides testimony to aid in social transformation, was exemplified by the numerous letter-writing campaigns whereby students conveyed their perspectives to outlets such as major media (p. 79).

Redemption in Lathan's model is not the religious quest for eternal salvation but a fierce commitment to "right-here-right-now liberation" (p. 24). Bernice Robinson stands as a prototype; she taught directly or indirectly, as Lathan notes, every teacher associated with the educational efforts of the Student Nonviolent Coordinating Committee, the Congress of Racial Equality, and the Southern Christian Leadership Conference (p. 111). It is little wonder, as Kynard suggests, that there was no shortage of Black activists ready to push for greater access and fairness in higher education and within the composition enterprise in particular.

As part of reimagining the landscape or textscape regarding African-American involvement with composition studies, we cannot ignore express concern for Black LGBTQ students and teachers, who within any sizeable assemblage of students are present—sometimes passively or actively but always *definitely*. This is a key message that Eric Darnell Pritchard (2017) conveys in *Fashioning Lives*. Grounded in his own lifelong encounters with both enabling and disabling aspects of literacy, and fortified by interviews with 60 LGBTQ subjects about their literacy practices, Pritchard theoretically shatters the paradigm of *literacy normativity* and cogently illustrates the need for a "framework through which literacy, composition, and rhetoric may see Black queerness generally and the theory [he develops] from the life stories of [his] participants in particular" (p. 13). For Pritchard, literacy normativity, the imposition of unjust standards, inflicts harm in its assault on the subjectivity of the designated "other." He advocates instead for *restorative literacies*; these consist of practices by Black queers that support "self-definition, self-care, and self-determination" (p. 24). Speaking to a disconnect between scholarship in literacy, composition, and rhetorical studies and Black LGBTQ experiences, he announces that part of his quest is

> to address the tyranny of literacy normativity as that thing that perpetually treats African American, LGBTQ literacy, composition, and rhetorical studies as mutually exclusive, which effectively makes it difficult, if not impossible, to speak to the intersections of these scholarly discourses in a way that gets us beyond what is a clear impasse so that work at the intersections of race, gender, sexuality, and queerness can be fully seen, heard and taken up.
>
> (p. 33)

With respect to writing classrooms, Pritchard suggests that race and sexuality be jointly considered in curricular design and course operation (p. 46). Matters to anticipate or attend to include homophobia in texts and teacher response, as well as the intersection of homophobia and race; the phenomena of sexuality and gender identity disclosures in student writing, or "coming out" by students or faculty; and the inclusion of materials that specifically reflect Black queer experiences so as not to perpetuate historical erasure (p. 45.). Like Kynard and Lathan, Pritchard views the Black Freedom Struggle as invaluable source material but has no use for a narrative of that valiant fight that continually elides Black queer contributions. Pritchard charges composition researches with the responsibility to conduct sexuality studies whether or not LGBTQ people are the focus; this is necessary he contends so that we don't treat sexuality as "other people's business" (p. 45). The best critical lens is the one that best aids our collective wisdom. The rigorous intersectional approach of a progressive "Black Queer Literacies" is for Pritchard, following the phrasing of poet Pat Parker, "a revolution" (p. 252).[5]

Of course, we have not been passive beings amid all this philosophizing and practice that gesture toward struggle and liberation. We have, in fact, both headed CCCC, the primary professional organization for college-writing studies, and we have been colleagues, acquaintances, or friends with every scholar featured in this chapter whose work dates from the 1960s onward. In addition, our own intellectual contributions run parallel to many of the scholarly developments described in this chapter and are complementary to them (Gilyard, 1991, 2011, 2016; Banks, 2006, 2011, 2015).

Gilyard, a transdisciplinary scholar, is known in composition studies for championing the idea of critical language awareness;[6] theorizing about race, identity, and politics; and stressing the value of African-American expressive culture, particularly African-American Vernacular English, in writing classrooms. In his education memoir *Voices of the Self* (1991), he argues that, across the length of the curriculum, schools should refrain from extracting severe psychic payments from students by trying to trap them in monolingualist ideology, thereby promoting "failure" for many. One of the ways that he assesses formal language instruction is through the frameworks of eradicationism, pluralism, and bidialectalism (pp. 70–4). He judges eradication, with its focus on extirpating so-called deficient language varieties, and bidialectalism, with its emphasis on role-playing, to be insufficient, if not catastrophic, responses to language diversity. Both approaches ultimately lend credence to deficit models and needlessly penalize students. For Gilyard, pluralism is the best path forward given its commitments to linguistic equality in schools and to social change beyond. However, Gilyard realizes that pluralism has not become a dominant pedagogy, not even among practitioners who share progressive language views. From his perspective, what has transpired instead is the code-switching paradigm, characterized by the following six tenets:

1. speech is a strong predictor of writing
2. codes are rather self-contained language systems linked to race and ethnicity
3. student identity is tied tightly to these codes
4. there are career benefits to switching between codes
5. this skill of switching can be taught
6. this skill of switching can be taught or at least facilitated in school
                    (*True to the Language Game*, 2011, p. 114)

He neither rejects the paradigm nor embraces it fully. Rather, he has focused on analyzing its strengths and weaknesses to guide further research.

In *True to the Language Game* (2011), Gilyard provides expansive remarks on language and politics, including an assessment of *Students' Right* and its reception (pp. 93–11), an intervention into the Ebonics controversy (pp. 52–7), and an interrogation of the link between Whiteness and composition studies (pp. 77–85), and the proffering of a vision of authentic democracy to which informed, critical, independent, and culturally sensitive student voices are central (pp. 12–21, 33–43, 258–69). He also provides glimpses of his work in classrooms as he pursues a critical-language-awareness agenda (pp. 172–8, 186–206). Moreover, because of his appreciation of transcultural conversation, he has interviewed a multicultural array of notable figures about a wide range of issues in Rhetoric and Composition, including, for example, Cornel West (2008, pp. 101–19). The list includes Steven Mailloux, C. Jan Swearingen, Jaime Armin Mejía, Haivan Hoang and LuMing Mao, Bronwyn Williams, Gwendolyn Pough, Jack Selzer, and David Kirkland (in Gilyard and Taylor, 2009, pp. 30–51, 54–71, 74–92, 106–24, 126–40, 142–55, 170–85, 224–43).

Banks has always spoken passionately about the value of African-American discursive traditions. Moreover, given his acute interest in design and technology issues, as well as in progress for African-American students and the communities from which they emerge, he has theoretically and practically blended African-American rhetoric, techno-discourse, critical pedagogy, and community work. In *Race, Rhetoric, and Technology* (2006), he suggests that if Rhetoric and Composition were construed as a community network, or perhaps "freenet," it would work against the tendency to valorize Standardized English at the expense of other valuable forms of expression (p. 85). Eschewing a deficit model, Banks believes that writing courses should be responsive to local situations and to various avenues to rhetorical excellence (p. 85). He also urges writing teachers to experiment with technology in their courses and provides concrete suggestions for how to do so (pp. 139–42).

In *Digital Griots* (2011), he ponders how African-American rhetorical traditions can best inform multimedia writing courses (p. 2) and settles on the figure of the DJ as the model for contemporary digital griots, who, in turn, are the embodiment of Black rhetorical virtuosity because of their commitment to craft and their abilities to carry and reinvigorate the old stories as well as to synthesize print, oral, and digital communication (pp. 25–6). He offers a list of specific writing practices that the work of DJs signify:

1.   the shoutout as the use of references, calling the roll, and identifying and declaring one's relationships, allegiances, and influences as tools for building community and locating oneself in it
2.   crate-digging as continual research—not merely for the songs, hooks, breakbeats, riffs, texts, arguments, and quotes for a particular set or paper but as a crucial part of one's long-term work, of learning, knowing, and interpreting a tradition
3.   mixing as the art of the transition and as revision in the Adrienne Rich sense of writing as re-vision[7]
4.   remix as critical interpretation of a text, repurposing it for a different rhetorical situation as 2010 Conference on College Composition and Communication chair Gwen Pough challenges the field to "remix: revisit, rethink, revise, renew" in the conference call[8]
5.   mixtape as anthology, as everyday act of canon formation, interpretation, and reinterpretation

6. sample as those quotes, those texts, those ideas used enough, important enough to our conceptions of what we are doing in a text (or even in our lifelong work) to be looped and continually repeated rather than merely quoted or referenced.

(p. 26)

Furthermore, Banks illustrates his pedagogical commitments in his description of a community-based, digital-griot writing curriculum that he orchestrated (pp. 55–85). In short, he has extended the progressive and enabling qualities that we mentioned at the outset of this chapter.

Notes

1. The conference, held at Dartmouth College, was a gathering of British and American educators. It was funded by the Carnegie Endowment and organized by the Modern Language Association and the National Council of Teachers of English.
2. The members of the committee, along with Butler, were Adam Casmier, Ninfa Flores, Jenefer Giannasi, Myrna Harrison, Robert Hogan, Richard Lloyd-Jones, Richard Long, Elizabeth Martin, Elisabeth McPherson, Nancy Pritchard, Geneva Smitherman, and Ross Winterowd.
3. For a second book-length treatise on the efficacy of rap for composition instruction, see David F. Green's doctoral dissertation, *It's Deeper than Rap: A Study of Hip Hop Music and Composition Pedagogy.*
4. In *Their Eyes Were Watching God* (1937), the character Janie, reflecting on the merit of her own travels, tells her best friend Pheoby Watson, "'Course, talkin' don't amount tuh uh hill uh beans when yuh can't do nothin' else. And listenin' tuh dat kind uh talk is jus' lak openin' yo' mouth and lettin' de moon shine down yo' throat. It's a known fact, Pheoby, you got tuh *go* there to *know* there. Yo' papa and yo' mama and nobody else can't tell yuh and show yuh. Two things everybody's got tuh do fuh theyselves. They got tuh go tuh God, and they got tuh find out about livin' fuh theyselves" (p. 285).
5. Pritchard is drawing on Parker's words in Battle et al. (2002): "If I could take all my parts with me when I go somewhere. And not have to say to one of them, "No, you stay home tonight, you won't be welcome," because I'm going to an all-White party where I can be gay, but not Black. Or I'm going to a Black poetry reading, and half the poets are anti-homosexual or thousands of situations where something of what I am cannot come with me. The day all the different parts of me can come along, we would have what I would call a revolution" (p. vi).
6. Romy Clark, Roz Ivanič, and their colleagues at Lancaster University coined the term *critical language awareness.*
7. See Rich's (1972) essay in *College English*, "When We Dead Awaken: Writing as Re-vision."
8. In her "Greetings from the 2010 Program Chair," Pough announced, "After decades of innovative teaching and cutting-edge scholarship, the 2010 conference is a space for us to revisit, rethink, revise and renew our vision for the future of the field" (p. 5).

8   Conclusion

Award-winning journalist Isabel Wilkerson, in a piece titled "Where Do We Go from Here?" described the enduring exigence of African-American rhetoric:

> Before the summer of 2014 . . . we may have lulled ourselves into believing that the struggle was over, that it had all been taken care of back in 1964, that the marching and bloodshed had established, once and for all, the basic rights of people who had been at the bottom for centuries. We may have believed that, if nothing else, the civil rights movement had defined a bar beneath which we could not fall.
>
> But history tells us otherwise. We seem to be in a continuing feedback loop of repeating a past that our country has yet to address. Our history is one of spectacular achievement (as in black senators of the Reconstruction era or the advances that culminated in the election of Barack Obama) followed by a violent backlash that threatens to erase the gains and then a long, slow climb to the next mountain, where the cycle begins again.
>
> (p. 59)

One way, then, to understand African-American rhetoric is as the study of how Black people in the United States have used discourse across all media and modalities to manage and try to escape this continuing feedback loop.

Perhaps one of the more remarkable and poignant recent examples of African-American rhetoric is not a speech or print document but this image of the activist known as France Francois. The text of her sign, the dedication in her stance, and the serious look on her face combine to exemplify a good deal of Black activism and public debate in this moment.

Francois held up the sign in 2014 during the National Moment of Silence,[1] an event held to express solidarity with activists in Ferguson protesting the death of Michael Brown at the hands of police. The image went viral and Francois has taken to Twitter (@1stClassFrance) and other forms of media as an advocate on matters beyond Ferguson. Her Twitter profile page

Figure 8.1

describes her as "linking the Black experience globally" (https://twitter.com/1stClassFrance accessed August 29, 2017), and her website provides the following biography:

> France Francois is a multifaceted writer, human rights activist and advocate for increasing global engagement amongst the diaspora while

building global platforms . . . to drive change. She is a product of the vibrant Haitian immigrant community of Miami. Passionate about the intersection of social inclusion, social justice, foreign aid, policy and immigration. . . . Most notably, as the founder of Rights for All in the Dominican Republic, she organized an international coalition to lobby against human rights violations in the Dominican Republic.

("About France Francois." Retrieved from
www.francefrancois.com/about).

This image points to the possibilities and limits of rhetoric for Black people in the United States, and it demonstrates the range of what study in Black rhetoric will have to attend to moving forward: a convergence of word, image, body, performance, and network; a merging of analog and digital discourse; and the interconnectedness of Black people in the United States and the worldwide African diaspora.

We close this book, in which we have considered the range of interconnected phenomena—individual exemplars to everyday folk, finished texts to ephemeral messages, explicitly persuasive discourse to informal communication that contributes to broader cultural frameworks, printed word to the performative and richly multimedia—with reflections on how the field of African-American rhetoric might continue to unfold. We indicate some thematic concerns as well as some areas of methodological need. This reflection resists any one narrative of closure and is far more about highlighting possibilities rather than drawing boundaries. We hope that students and scholars taking up our call will push it far beyond what we might imagine.

There is a need for increased scholarly attention to composing practices employed by Black rhetors in out-of-school settings. What might we learn from a study of the speechwriters who worked with Michelle Obama during her time as First Lady? What is to be gleaned from an exploration of Black workers in STEM fields who must constantly negotiate their expertise in their fields with the realities of being a Black woman or man, trans or cisgender in those industries? What communication practices do they use in that negotiation and how do these realities influence their composing processes? What do Black digital-content creators do when they look to create the next meme or video or blog post that they hope will go viral or at least become influential? Composing practices and processes are essential for their own sake but also central to rhetorical study.

Some other thematic impulses that need far more attention in the published scholarship involve African-American rhetoric in conversation with other traditions. Over the last fifty years, we have seen the pronounced emergence of a U.S.-based Black population that cannot be contained or described simply as African-American in the traditional sense. This shift has created a need to examine what we have called African-American rhetoric in conversation with African, Caribbean, Afro-Latinx, and

Afro-European traditions and to explore the ways that population shifts in the United States have influenced contemporary African-American rhetorical practices. During the 2007 version of The State of the Black Union,[2] an annual convention organized by Tavis Smiley, long-time artist and activist Harry Belafonte challenged audience members to move beyond the borders of the nation-state in terms of claiming their identity. Belafonte noted that not only did historical circumstances of enslavement complicate understandings of Black American identity as fully distinct from that of Black people in Jamaica or Cuba or Brazil, for example, but that Black people throughout the Caribbean, Central America, and South America were eager to work together with African Americans in a quest for liberation that would extend beyond any one nation's borders. To Belafonte's point, while African-American history, identity, and freedom struggles have very specific contours given the strange crucible of the American experiment, African-American life and thus rhetoric cannot be contained by that crucible.

A related but distinct need in African-American rhetorical study and scholarship is for cross conversation between African-American rhetoric and what we might identify as other ethnic rhetorics. The last two decades have witnessed an emergence of more scholarship in areas like Latinx, Asian, Asian-American, and Indigenous rhetorics. We can learn from studying these areas in their own right and studying them in connection with each other and with African-American rhetoric.

Furthermore, there is need for far more work at the intersection of Black rhetorical traditions and technology issues. Scholarship taking up questions of technology and rhetoric need to understand technology(ies) as a site of inquiry rather than as merely a site of production of discourse. While the importance of attending to a wide range of media and modalities for the study of rhetoric has been compellingly demonstrated through technology innovation on #BlackTwitter, meme culture, and other means, we also want to emphasize the ways that technologies and technology issues contribute to the structural conditions of Black life and are themselves a site of struggle. Rhetoric and its production are not merely limited to human agents: "bots" programmed to carry out certain communication functions and algorithms contribute to the contexts in which people communicate and therefore have consequences in people's lives.

In *Algorithms of Oppression: How Search Engines Reinforce Racism* (2018), communications scholar Safiya Noble calls for students and scholars to attend to "digital redlining." She highlights the ways people are organizing to intervene in response to this evolving form of racial discrimination:

> Interventions like Black Girls Code, an organization focused on teaching young, African American girls to program, is the kind of intervention we see building in response to the ways Black women have been locked out of

Silicon Valley venture capital and broader participation. Simultaneously, it is important for the public, particularly people who are marginalized—like women and girls, and people of color—to be critical of the results that purport to represent them in the first ten to twenty results of a commercial search engine.

(p. 26)

Noble stresses the importance of gaining knowledge of the technical aspects of search and retrieval and the necessity of learning to critique the computer programming codes that underlie systems (p. 26).

We long ago reached the point where the distinction people used to draw between our online interactions and IRL (in real life) can no longer be realistically made: There is truly nothing we do in our offline lives that is not also part of online connections and communication. And the realities of our continually merging relationships with technologies extend beyond communication. We close this volume amid speculation that the next version of the Apple iPhone will include facial recognition software and with news reports that a software development company called Three Square Market is inviting its workers to volunteer to have Radio Frequency ID microchips implanted in their hands. As Marks (2017) notes, employees will be able to "open doors, pay for purchases, share business cards, store medical information, pay for stuff at other RFID terminals and login to their computers . . . all with a wave of a hand."

Our relationships with technologies in this era in which people debate whether or not we have become "posthuman" or "transhuman" are every bit as crucial to the conditions of Black lives and the ways in which people live them as are the legal system, conditions of employment, policing, education, entertainment, and recreation. These relationships with technologies are central to the study of rhetoric.

Similarly, in an era of information overload as a part of daily life, archiving and curation—and being able to work with archives of various sorts—become crucial elements of rhetorical study and thus study in African-American rhetoric as well. There are many practices and artifacts that should be collected, preserved, and curated for study and analysis both now and in the future, and there is significant work to do with Black archives in many different spaces from university collections to those in boxes in a family's attic or the basement of an organization's building. In a digital age, so many kinds of communication that are crucial to any particular moment will fade given the ephemeral nature of sites, servers, and services that come and go at a moment's notice. The video looping site Vine provides an instructive example. In late October 2016, Vine's founders notified the public that the site would be discontinued despite its popularity and the ways it changed part of digital culture. The suddenness of the announcement caused a significant amount of dismay for users and fans, resulting in debate and instant nostalgia through hashtags like #RIPVine. As fleeting as six seconds of looping video are, the millions and millions of Vines people posted demonstrated that the site changed the act of using video to tell stories. Vine was especially known as a space for both Black humor and advocacy as the combination of the constraint of six seconds and the possibility of infinite repetition through the looping feature was embraced by activists and cut-ups alike.

Meme culture provides another example of a communication practice that would benefit from careful archiving and curation of even representative samples so that future students and scholars could study them, both in real time and across time when communication technologies, needs, and practices change. We mention Vine and meme culture to highlight the serious need for significant work in African-American visual rhetorics, from our current moment back throughout all periods of Black life in this society. We have no book-length formal study of African-American visual rhetorics, and such a project is way overdue.

No matter the forms people use, however, from memes to Vines to tweets to speeches, sermons or songs, there is a need for more physical and print archives designed for rhetorical study. The History of Black Writing Project, housed at the University of Kansas, provides an excellent example of how rhetorical texts and productions within and across genres, media, and modalities might be archived for contemporary and long-term study.

We have been intentionally broad in this closing sketch about the kinds of work that we hope students and scholars in African-American rhetoric will pursue in the near future. If there is anything that the study of African-American rhetoric should make clear, it is that hagiographic, exemplar-driven studies of rhetoric focused solely on the spoken or written word are not sufficient to the task. Even when it is necessary to build from examples, no matter how instructive they might be, they are never sufficient for the range of aims, audiences, arguments, appeals and aesthetics that we find in even a single day of Black rhetorical production, much less in an era defined by "streaming," always on, information. Thus, any study, even with methods and theoretical commitments that focus on broad communities and masses of people instead of simply notable individuals, can only be suggestive rather than definitive, can only be a call that hopes for response. That is what we hope our book offers—a call that sounds out some of what has been done, a sense of just how much is possible, and a gesture toward future directions for the study of African-American rhetoric amid the plethora of voices, networks, movements, and spaces that students and scholars might explore together. Given the reality of constant change and a constantly quickening tempo of change in what are already overwhelmingly fast and voluminous forms of rhetorical production, we all need to be archivists as well as analysts in the work ahead. We all need to be curators as much as commentators, working to save, sample, and Storify the range of compelling efforts in our midst and in our history as part of how we work through the complexities of Black rhetoric in the pursuit of life, love, and liberation, across all the intersections, convergences, and differences that mark any community, but especially Black communities at this moment in time.

Notes

1. The National Moment of Silence for Victims of Police Brutality was a wave of vigils held in more than 90 cities on August 14, 2014. See www.huffingtonpost. com/2014/08/15/national-moment-of-silence-nmos14_n_5682170.html
2. In 2010, after a decade of events, Smiley announced The State of the Black Union would no longer be convened.

References

Ajayi, L. (2015). Retrieved from www.awesomelyluvvie.com/2015/11/thanksgiving-clapback-hashtag.html

Alexander, M. (2012). *The new Jim Crow: Mass incarceration in the age of colorblindness.* Rev. edition. New York: The New Press.

Anderson, E. (1985). Using folk literature in teaching composition. In Brooks, C. (Ed.), *Tapping potential: English and language arts for the Black learner* (pp. 219–25). Urbana, IL: National Council of Teachers of English.

Aristotle. (1989). *Prior analytics.* (R. Smith, Trans.). Indianapolis: Hackett Publishing Company.

Aristotle. (2006). *On rhetoric: A theory of civic discourse.* 2nd edition. (G. A. Kennedy, Trans.). New York: Oxford University Press.

Asante, M. K. [published as Smith, A. L.]. (1969). *Rhetoric of Black revolution.* Boston: Allyn and Bacon.

Asante, M. K. [published as Smith, A. L.]. (1972). *Language, communication, and rhetoric in Black America.* New York: Harper & Row.

Asante, M. K. (1998). *The Afrocentric idea.* Rev. edition. Philadelphia: Temple University Press.

Asante, M. K. (2005). *Race, rhetoric, and identity: The architecton of soul.* Amherst, NY: Humanity Books.

Asante, M. K. (2016). *Lynching Barack Obama: How Whites tried to string up the president.* New York: Universal Write Publications LLC.

Asante, M. K. [published as Smith, A. L.], & Robb, S. (Eds.). (1971). *The voice of Black rhetoric.* Boston: Allyn and Bacon.

Atwater, D. F. (2009). *African American women's rhetoric: The search for dignity, personhood, and honor.* Lanham, MD: Rowman & Littlefield.

Bailey, Moya (2010) "They Aren't Talking About Me." Crunk Feminist Collective Blog. March 14, 2010.

Baker, E., & Cooke, M. (1935, November). The Bronx slave market. *Crisis,* 330–2.

Baldwin, J. (1957/1995). Sonny's blues. In *Going to meet the man* (pp. 101–41). New York: Vintage.

Baldwin, J. (1963). *The fire next time.* New York: Dell.

Bambara, T. C. (1972/1992). The lesson. In *Gorilla, my love* (pp. 85–96). New York: Vintage.

Bambara, T. C. (1995). The golden bandit. In Goss, L. & Goss, C. (Eds.), *Jump and say! A collection of Black storytelling* (pp. 207–10). New York: Touchstone.

Banks, A. J. (2006). *Race, rhetoric, and technology: Searching for higher ground*. Mahwah, NJ: Lawrence Erlbaum Associates and the National Council of Teachers of English.

Banks, A. J. (2011). *Digital Griots: African American rhetoric in a multimedia age*. Carbondale, IL: Southern Illinois University Press.

Banks, A. J. (2015). Ain't no walls behind the sky, baby! Funk, flight, freedom. CCC, 67(2), 267–79.

Baraka, A. (1966/1991). The changing same (R & B and new Black music). In Harris, W. J. (Ed.), *The LeRoi Jones/Amiri Baraka reader* (pp. 186–209). New York: Thunder's Mouth Press.

Barthes, R. (1988). *The semiotic challenge*. (R. Howard, Trans.). Oxford: Basil Blackwell.

Battle, J., Cohen, C., Warren, D., Ferguson, G., & Audam, S. (Eds.). (2002). *"Say it loud, I'm Black and I'm proud": Black pride survey 2000*. National Gay and Lesbian Policy Institute. Retrieved from www.thetaskforce.org/static_html/downloads/reports/SayItLoudBlackAndProud.pdf

Belafonte, H. (1954). John Henry. On *Mark Twain & other favorites* (LP). New York: RCA Victor.

Bell, B. W. (1987). *The Afro-American novel and its tradition*. Amherst, MA: University of Massachusetts Press.

Bethune, M. M. (1944). Certain unalienable rights. In Logan, R. W. (Ed.), *What the Negro wants* (pp. 248–58). Chapel Hill, NC: The University of North Carolina Press.

BET Staff. (2017a). *BET says to Black in joint Twitter study of Black Twitter*. Retrieved from www.bet.com/shows/upfront/news/2017/04/bet-networks-says-yes-to-comedy-superstars-and-music-legends.html

BET Staff. (2017b). *Everything you should know about BET's Twitter partnership*. Retrieved from www.bet.com/news/national/2017/05/22/everything-you-should-know-about-bet-s-twitter-partnership.html

Big Bill Broonzy. (1956). John Henry. On *Big Bill Broonzy sings folk songs* [LP]. Washington, DC: Smithsonian Folkways Recordings.

A Black feminist statement. (1978/2009). In James, S. M., Foster, F. S., & Guy-Sheftall, B. (Eds.), *Still brave: The evolution of Black women's studies* (pp. 3–11). New York: The Feminist Press.

BlogXilla. (2016). [Interview with Denzel Washington]. *Global Grind*. Retrieved from www.youtube.com/watch?v=dtoVILBa75I

Bonilla, Y., & Rosa, J. (2015, February) #Ferguson: Digital protest, hashtag ethnography, and the racial politics of social media in the United States. *American Ethnologist*, 4–17.

Branch, T. (2006). *At Canaan's edge: America in the King years, 1965–68*. New York: Simon & Schuster.

Brock, A. (2012). From the Blackhand side: Twitter as a cultural conversation. *Journal of Broadcasting & Electronic Media*, 56, 529–49.

Brooks, C. (Ed.). (1985). *Tapping potential: English and language arts for the Black learner*. Urbana, IL: National Council of Teachers of English.

Brown, H. Q. (1880). *Bits and odds: A choice selection of recitations*.

Brown, H. Q. (1910). *Elocution and physical culture: Training for students, teachers, readers, public speakers*. Wilberforce, OH: Homewood Cottage.

Brown, H. Q. (1975). First lessons in public speaking. In A. S. McFarlin, *Hallie Quinn Brown: Black woman elocutionist* (pp. 156–72). (Doctoral dissertation), Washington State University.

Brown, J. (1968). Advanced composition. *CLA Journal*, 12(1), 26–31.

Browne, S. (2015). *Dark matters: On the surveillance of Blackness*. Durham, NC: Duke University Press.

Burke, K. (1941). Four master tropes. *The Kenyon Review* (Autumn), 421–38.

Burke, K. (1984). *Attitudes toward history*. 3rd edition. Berkeley: University of California Press.

Butler, M. (1971). The implications of Black dialect for teaching English in predominantly Black colleges. *CLA Journal*, 15(2), 235–9.

Byerman, K. E. (1985). *Fingering the jagged grain: Tradition and form in recent Black fiction*. Athens, GA: University of Georgia Press.

Caesar, S. (1988/2011). Hold my mule. On *The ultimate collection* [CD]. Nashville: Word Entertainment.

Callahan, A. D. (2008). *The talking book: African Americans and the Bible*. New Haven, CT: Yale University Press.

Campbell, B., & Austin, E. A. (Eds.). (2013). *Mothership: Tales from Afrofuturism and beyond*. College Park, MD: Rosarium Publishing.

Campbell, K. E. (2005). *"Gettin' our groove on": Rhetoric, language, and literacy for the hip hop generation*. Detroit: Wayne State University Press.

Carmichael, S. (1966, September 22). What we want. *New York Review of Books*, 5–6, 8.

Carmichael, S. (with Ekwueme Michael Thelwell). (2003). *Ready for revolution: The life and struggles of Stokely Carmichael (Kwame Ture)*. New York: Scribner.

Carmichael, S., & Hamilton, C. V. (1967). *Black power: The politics of liberation in America*. New York: Vintage.

Clark, M. D. (2014). *To tweet our own cause: A mixed-methods study of the online phenomenon "Black Twitter"*. (Doctoral dissertation), The University of North Carolina.

Clark, R., & Ivanič, R. (1997). *The politics of writing*. London: Routledge.

Clegg, C. A., III. (1997). *An original man: The life and times of Elijah Muhammad*. New York: St. Martin's.

Cone, J. H. (1992). *The spirituals and the blues: An interpretation*. Maryknoll, NY: Orbis.

Cook, W. W. (1993). Writing in the spaces left. *College Composition and Communication*, 44(1), 9–25.

Cooper, A. J. (1892/1988). *A voice from the south*. New York: Oxford University Press.

Cooper, B.C., Morris, S. M., & Boylorn, R. M. (2017). Crunk glossary. In Cooper, B. C, Morris, S. M., & Boylorn, R. M. (Eds.) *The crunk feminist collective* (pp. 325–329). New York: Feminist Press.

Corbett, E. P. J. (Ed.). (1974). Students' right to their own language. [Special issue] *College Composition and Communication*, 25(3).

Cruse, H. (1967/1984). *The crisis of the Negro intellectual: A historical analysis of the failure of Black leadership*. New York: Quill.

Dalby, D. (1972). The African element in American English. In Kochman, T. (Ed.), *Rappin' and stylin' out: Communication in urban Black America* (pp. 170–86). Chicago: University of Illinois Press.

Dance, D. C. (2002a). The signifying monkey. In Dance, D. C. (Ed.), *From my people: 400 years of African American folklore* (pp. 492–4). New York: W. W. Norton.

Dance, D. C. (2002b). Stagolee. In Dance, D. C. (Ed.), *From my people: 400 years of African American folklore* (pp. 489–90). New York: W. W. Norton.

Davis, A. Y. (1999). *Blues legacies and Black feminism: Gertrude "Ma" Rainey, Bessie Smith, and Billie Holiday*. New York: Vintage.

Davis, A. Y. (2016). *Freedom is a constant struggle*. Chicago: Haymarket Books.

Davis, V. (1985). Teachers as editors: The student conference. In Brooks, C. (Ed.), *Tapping potential: English and language arts for the Black learner* (pp. 187–99). Urbana, IL: National Council of Teachers of English.

De La Soul. (1996). Stakes is high. On *Stakes is high* [LP]. New York: Tommy Boy Records.

de Man, P. (1979). *Allegories of reading: Figural language in Rousseau, Nietzsch, Rilke, and Proust*. New Haven, CT: Yale University Press.

de Man, P. (1982). The resistance to theory. *Yale French Studies*, 63, 3–20.

de Man, P. (1986). *Blindness and insight: Essays in the rhetoric of contemporary criticism*. London: Routledge.

Derrida, J. (2004). *Dissemination*. (B. Johnson, Trans.). London: Continuum.

Douglass, F. (1845). *Narrative of the life of Frederick Douglass, an American slave, written by himself*.

Douglass, F. (1848/1950). The blood of the slave on the skirts of the Northern people. *The North Star*. In Foner, P. S. (Ed.), *The life and writings of Frederick Douglass, volume 1, early years, 1817–1849* (pp. 343–7). New York: International.

Douglass, F. (1850/1982). Is the Constitution pro-slavery? A debate between Frederick Douglass, Charles C. Burleigh, Gerrit Smith, Parker Pillsbury, Samuel Ringgold Ward, and Stephen S. Foster in Syracuse, New York, on 17 January 1850. In Blassingame, J. W. (Ed.), *The Frederick Douglass papers, series one, speeches, debates, and interviews, volume 3, 1855–1863* (pp. 217–35). New Haven: Yale University Press.

Douglass, F. (1855/1968). *My bondage and my freedom*. New York: Arno.

Douglass, F. (1857/1985). Colored men's rights in this republic: An address delivered in New York, New York, on 14 May 1857. In Blassingame, J. W. (Ed.), *The Frederick Douglass papers, series one, speeches, debates, and interviews, volume 3, 1855–1863* (pp. 143–50). New Haven: Yale University Press.

Douglass, F. (1860/1985). The American Constitution and the slave: An address delivered in Glasgow, Scotland, on 26 March 1860. In Blassingame, J. W. (Ed.), *The Frederick Douglass papers, series one, speeches, debates, and interviews, volume 3, 1855–1863* (pp. 340–66). New Haven: Yale University Press.

Du Bois, W. E. B. (1897/1996). The conservation of races. In Sundquist, E. J. (Ed.), *The Oxford W. E. B. Du Bois reader* (pp. 38–47). New York: Oxford University Press.

Du Bois, W. E. B. (1903/1994). Of the coming of John. In *The souls of Black folk* (pp. 141–53). Mineola, NY: Dover.

Du Bois, W. E. B. (1906/1996). The Niagara movement. In Sundquist, E. J. (Ed.), *The Oxford W. E. B. Du Bois reader* (pp. 373–6). New York: Oxford University Press.

Du Bois, W. E. B. (1917/1996). Awake America. In Sundquist, E. J. (Ed.), *The Oxford W. E. B. Du Bois reader* (p. 379). New York: Oxford University Press.

Du Bois, W. E. B. (1926, October). Criteria of Negro Art. *Crisis*, 290–7.

Du Bois, W. E. B. (1934, November). [Headnote]. *Crisis*, 327.

Dunbar, P. L. (1895/1993). We wear the mask. In Braxton, J. M. (Ed.), *The collected poetry of Paul Laurence Dunbar* (p. 71). Charlottesville, VA: University Press of Virginia.

Dunbar, P. L. (1896/1993). Ode to Ethiopia. In Braxton, J. M. (Ed.), *The collected poetry of Paul Laurence Dunbar* (pp. 15–16). Charlottesville, VA: University of Virginia Press.

Durham, A. (2007). Using [living hip-hop] feminism: Redefining an answer (to) rap. In Pough, G. D., Richardson, E., Durham, A., & Raimist, R. (Eds.), *Home girls make some noise: Hip hop feminism anthology* (pp. 304–12). Mira Loma, CA: Parker Publishing.

Eglash, R. (2004). Appropriating technology: An introduction. In Eglash, R., Croissant, J. L., Di Chiro, G., & Fouché, R. (Eds.), *Appropriating technology: Vernacular science and social power* (pp. vii–xxi). Minneapolis: University of Minnesota Press.

Ellis, E. G. (2017, March 1). Want to profit of your meme? Good luck if you aren't White. *Wired*. Retrieved from wired.com

Ellison, R. (1952/1995). *Invisible man*. New York: Vintage.

Epps, J. (1985). Killing them softly: Why Willie can't write. In Brooks, C. (Ed.), *Tapping potential: English and language arts for the Black learner* (pp. 154–8). Urbana, IL: National Council of Teachers of English.

Equiano, O. (1789/1995). *The interesting narrative of the life of Olaudah Equiano, or Gustavus Vassa, the African, written by himself*. In Carretta, V. (Ed.), *The interesting narrative and other writings* (pp. 1–236). New York: Penguin.

Eve. (1999). Love is blind. On *Let there be Eve . . . Ruff Ryders' first lady* [LP]. Santa Monica, CA: Interscope.

Fisher, D., & Stepto, R. B. (Eds.). (1979). *Afro-American literature: The reconstruction of instruction*. New York: Modern Language Association.

Florini, S. (2014). Tweets, tweeps, and signifyin': Communication and cultural performance on "Black Twitter." *Television & News Media*, 15, 223–37.

Foner, P. S., & Branham, R. J. (Eds.). (1998). *Lift every voice: African American Oratory, 1787–1900* (pp. 226–9). Tuscaloosa, AL: The University of Alabama Press.

Foucault, M. (1969/1972). *The archaeology of knowledge and the discourse on language*. (A. M. S. Smith, Trans.). New York: Pantheon.

Franklin, K. (1997). Stomp. On *God's property* [CD]. Santa Monica, CA: Interscope.

Freelon, D., McIlwain, C. D., & Clark, M. D. (2016). *Beyond the hashtags: #Ferguson, #BlackLivesMatter, and the online struggle for offline justice*. Washington, DC: Center for Media & Social Impact, School of Communication, American University.

Freire, P. (1970). *Pedagogy of the oppressed*. (M. B. Ramos, Trans.). New York: Continuum.

Friedman, J. L. (2015). *Music in our lives: Why we listen, how it works*. Jefferson, NC: McFarland & Company.

Fugees. (1996). The mask. On *The Score* [CD]. Philadelphia: Ruffhouse Records.

Gaines, E. (1964). *Catherine Carmier*. New York: Atheneum.

Gaines, E. (1971). *The autobiography of Miss Jane Pitman*. New York: Doubleday.

Garrity-Blake, B. (2004). Raising fish with song: Technology, chanteys, and African-Americans in the Atlantic menhaden fishery. In Sinclair, B. (Ed.), *Technology and the African-American experience: Needs and opportunities for study* (pp. 107–17). Cambridge, MA: The MIT Press.

Garvey, M. (1923/1986). Africa for the Africans. In Garvey, A. J. (Ed.), *The philosophy and opinions of Marcus Garvey* (pp. 68–72). Dover, MA: The Majority Press.

Gates, H. L., Jr. (1987). *Figures in Black: Words, signs, and the "racial" self*. New York: Oxford University Press.

Gates, H. L., Jr. (1988a). *The signifying monkey: A theory of Afro-American literary criticism*. New York: Oxford University Press.

Gates, H. L., Jr. (1988b). The trope of a New Negro and the reconstruction of the image of the Black. *Representations*, 24, 129–55.

Gates, H. L., Jr. (1998). The talking book. In Gates, H. L., Jr. & Andrews, W. L. (Eds.), *Pioneers of the Black Atlantic: Five slave narratives from the enlightenment, 1772–1815* (pp. 1–29). Washington, DC: Civitas.

Gaye, M. (1973). Just to keep you satisfied. On *Let's get it on* [LP]. Los Angeles: Tamla Records.

Gee, J. P. (1988). The legacies of literacy: From Plato to Freire through Harvey Graff. *Harvard Educational Review*, 58, 195–212.

Geismar. P. (1971). *Fanon*. New York: Dial.

Genette, G. (1982). *Figures of literary discourse*. (A. Sheridan, Trans.). Oxford: Basil Blackwell.

Gibson, D. (1989). Introduction. In *The souls of Black folk* (pp. xi–xv). New York: Penguin.

Giddings, P. (1984). *When and where I enter: The impact of Black women on race and sex in America*. New York: William Morrow and Company.

Gilyard, K. (1991). *Voices of the self: A study of language competence*. Detroit: Wayne State University Press.

Gilyard, K. (1996). *Let's flip the script: An African American discourse on language, literature, and learning*. Detroit: Wayne State University Press.

Gilyard, K. (2008). *Composition and Cornel West: Notes toward a deep democracy*. Carbondale, IL: Southern Illinois University Press.

Gilyard, K. (2010). *John Oliver Killens: A life of Black literary activism*. Athens, GA: University of Georgia Press.

Gilyard, K. (2011). *True to the language game: African American discourse, cultural politics, and pedagogy*. New York: Routledge.

Gilyard, K. (2016). The rhetoric of translingualism. *College English*, 78(3), 284–9.

Gilyard, K., & Taylor, V. E. (2009). *Conversations in cultural rhetoric and composition studies*. Aurora, CO: The Davies Group Publishers.

Go down, Moses. (1998). In Hill, P. L., Bell, B. W., Harris, W. J., Miller, R. B., O'Neale, S. A., & Porter, H. (Eds.), *The Riverside anthology of the African American literary tradition* (pp. 42–4). Boston: Houghton Mifflin.

God's going to trouble the water. (2004). In Gilyard, K. & Wardi, A. (Eds.), *African American literature* (p. 122). New York: Penguin Academics.

Gordon, D. B. (2003). *Black identity: Rhetoric, ideology, and nineteenth-century Black nationalism*. Carbondale, IL: Southern Illinois University Press.

Gramsci, A. (1971). The intellectuals. In Hoare, Q. & Smith, G. N. (Eds.), *Selections from the prison notebooks of Antonio Gramsci*. (Q. Hoare & N. V. Smith, Trans.) (pp. 5–23). New York: International.

Green, D. F. (2011). *It's deeper than rap: A study of hip hop music and composition pedagogy*. (Doctoral dissertation), The Pennsylvania State University.

Griggs, S. E. (1899/2003). *Imperium in imperio*. New York: The Modern Library.

Gronniosaw, J. A. U. (1770/1998). A narrative of the most remarkable particulars in the life of James Albert Ukawsaw Gronniosaw, an African prince, as related by himself. In Gates, H. L., Jr. & Andrews, W. L. (Eds.), *Pioneers of the Black Atlantic: Five slave narratives from the enlightenment, 1772–1815* (pp. 30–59). Washington, DC: Civitas.

Haley, A. (1965). Epilogue. In Malcolm X (with Alex Haley), *The autobiography of Malcolm X* (pp. 390–466). New York: Grove.

Hamilton, V. (1985/2004). *The people could fly*. New York: Knopf.

Hamner, C. (2012). *The disaster of innovation*. Retrieved from Teachinghistory.org

Hansberry, L. (1959/2004). *A raisin in the sun*. New York: Vintage.

Harper, F. E. W. (1854/1988). Ethiopia. In *Complete poems of Frances E. W. Harper* (pp. 7–8). New York: Oxford University Press.

Higginbotham, E. B. (1993). *Righteous discontent: The women's movement in the Black Baptist church, 1880–1920*. Cambridge, MA: Harvard University Press.

Hill, P. L., Bell, B. W., Harris, W. J., Miller, R. B., O'Neale, S. A., & Porter, H. (Eds.). (1998). *The Riverside anthology of the African American literary tradition*. Boston: Houghton Mifflin.

Himes, C. (1945/2002). *If he hollers let him go.* New York: Thunder's Mouth Press.

Himes, C. (1969/1989). *Blind man with a pistol.* New York: Vintage.

Holloway, J. E., & Vass, W. K. (1993). *The African heritage of American English.* Bloomington, IN: Indiana University Press.

hooks, b. (1981). *Ain't I a woman: Black women and feminism.* Boston: South End Press.

Howard-Pitney, D. (1990). *The Afro-American jeremiad: Appeals for justice in America.* Philadelphia: Temple University Press.

Howell, P. (2016, October 27). How Barry Jenkins gave voice to his past in *Moonlight.* *Toronto Star.*

Hudson-Weems, C. (1994). *Africana womanism: Reclaiming ourselves.* Troy, MI: Bedford Publishers.

Hughes, L. (1920/1994). The Negro speaks of rivers. In Rampersad, A. & Roessel, D. (Eds.), *The collected poetry of Langston Hughes* (p. 23). New York: Vintage.

Humphrey, H. (1966/1969). Address at the NAACP convention, July 6, 1966. In Scott, R. & Brockriede, W. (Eds.), *The rhetoric of Black power* (pp. 65–73). New York: Harper & Row.

Hurston, Z. N. (1937/1978). *Their eyes were watching God.* Urbana, IL: University of Illinois Press.

Ice Cube, Woods-Wright, T., Alvarez, M., Gray, F. G., Bernstein, S., Dr. Dre (Producers), & Gray, F. C. (Director). (2015). *Straight outta Compton.* New York: Universal.

Jackson, G. P. (1932, June). The genesis of the Negro spiritual. *The American Mercury,* 243–9.

Jackson, R., Jr., & Macedon, D. (Writers), & McKay, J. (Director). (2015). Time's up. [Television series episode]. In Kemp, C. A., Knoller, D., Jackson, C., Canton, M., Emmett, R., & Rainey, M., Jr. (Producers). *Power.* New York, NY: Starz Originals.

Jacobs, H. (1861/1973). *Incidents in the life of a slave girl.* San Diego: Harcourt Brace & Company.

Janelle Monáe and the Wondaland Artist Collective. (2015). *Hell you talmbout.* [Digital File]. Atlanta: Wondaland Records.

Ja Rule. (2003). Clap back. On *Blood in my eye* [CD]. New York: Murder Inc. Records.

John Henry. (1971). In Randall, D. (Ed.), *The Black poets* (pp. 12–15). New York: Bantam.

John in jail. (1976). In Courlander, H. (Ed.), *A treasury of Afro-American folklore: The oral literature, traditions, recollections, legends, tales, songs, religious beliefs, customs, sayings and humor of peoples of African descent in the Americas* (p. 44). New York: Marlowe & Company.

Johnson, J. W. (1931/1969). Preface to the first edition. In Johnson, J. W. (Ed.), *The book of American Negro poetry* (pp. 9–48). San Diego: Harcourt Brace & Company.

Jones, C. (1949, June). An end to the neglect of the problems of the Negro woman! *Political Affairs,* 3–19.

Jones, T. (2014). *Big data and Black Twitter.* Retrieved from www.languagejones.com/ blog-1/2014/9/26/big-data-and-black-twitter

Joshua fit de battle of Jericho. (1998). In Newman, R. (Ed.), *Go down, Moses: A celebration of the African-American spiritual* (p. 94). New York: Clarkson/Potter.

Karger, M. (Director). (1921). *Message from Mars.* Los Angeles: Metro Pictures Corporation.

Keats, E. J. (1965). *John Henry: An American legend.* New York: Knopf.

Kelly, E. (1968). Murder of the American dream. *CCC,* 19(2), 106–8.

Kendrick Lamar. (2015). Alright. On *To pimp a butterfly* [CD]. Carson, CA: Top Dawg/ Aftermath/Interscope.

Killens, J. O. (1954/1982). *Youngblood*. Athens, GA: University of Georgia Press.

Killens, J. O. (1975). *A man ain't nothin' but a man: The adventures of John Henry*. Boston: Little, Brown and Company.

Killer Mike. (2014, November 24). [Speech]. Retrieved from www.youtube.com/watch?v=MQs7CWKHM9w

King, M. L., Jr. (1963/1986). I have a dream. In Washington, J. M. (Ed.), *A testament of hope: The essential writings of Martin Luther King, Jr.* (pp. 217–20). San Francisco: Harper.

King, M. L., Jr. (1968). *Where do we go from here: Chaos or community?* Boston: Beacon.

Knight, E. (1968). Hard Rock returns to prison from the hospital for the criminal insane. In *Poems from prison* (pp. 11–12). Detroit: Broadside Press.

Knight, E. (1968/2004). Dark prophecy: I sing of Shine. In Gilyard, K. & Wardi, A. (Eds.), *African American literature* (pp. 377–8). New York: Penguin Academics.

Kurtis Blow. (1980). The breaks. On *Kurtis Blow* [LP]. New York: Mercury.

Kynard, C. (2013). *Vernacular insurrections: Race, Black protest, and the new century in composition-literacies studies*. Albany, NY: State University of New York Press.

Lathan, R. E. (2015). *Freedom writing: African American civil rights literacy activism, 1955–1967*. Conference on College Composition and Communication and the National Council of Teachers of English. Urbana, IL.

Lead Belly. (1994). John Henry. On *Lead Belly's last sessions* [CD]. Washington, DC: Smithsonian Folkways Recordings.

LeClair, T. (1981, March 21). "The language must not sweat": A conversation with Toni Morrison. *The New Republic*, 25–9.

Lil Jon and the Eastside Boyz. (2002). Get low. On *Kings of crunk* [CD]. New York: TVT Records.

Linthwaite, I. (Ed.). (1988). *Ain't I a woman! A book of women's poetry from around the world*. New York: Peter Bedrick Books.

Locke, A. (1925). The New Negro. In Locke, A. (Ed.), *The New Negro: An interpretation* (pp. 3–16). New York: Albert and Charles Boni.

Malcolm X. (1964). *The ballot or the bullet*. Retrieved from www.youtube.com/watch?v=ffqVJWP5OeU

Malcolm X (with Alex Haley). (1965a). *The autobiography of Malcolm X*. New York: Grove.

Malcolm X. (1965b). The ballot or the bullet. In *Malcolm X speaks* (pp. 23–44). New York: Pathfinder.

Malcolm X. (1971). God's judgment of White America (the chickens are coming home to roost). In Karim, B. (Ed.), *The end of White world supremacy: Four speeches by Malcolm X* (pp. 121–48). New York: Arcade Publishing.

Mandigo, A. (1999). Do the ratchet. On *Ratchet fight in the ghetto* [CD]. Shreveport, LA: Lava House Records.

Manjoo, F. (2010, August 10). *How Black people use Twitter: The latest research on race and micro blogging*. Retrieved from www.slate.com/articles/technology/technology/2010/08/how_black_people_use_twitter.html

Margouleff, R. (2012). *"I thought he was a messenger": Making Stevie Wonder's "Talking book"*. Retrieved from www.theatlantic.com/entertainment/archive/2012/10/i-thought-he-was-a-messenger-making-stevie-wonders-talking-book/264182/

Marks, G. (2017, July 24). A Wisconsin company offers to implant remote control microchips in its employees. *Washington Post*. Retrieved from www.washingtonpost.

com/news/digger/wp/2017/07/24/a-u-s-company-offers-to-implant-chips-in-its-employees/?utm_term=.baec8f9e83

Marley, B. (1979). Africa unite. On *Survival* [LP]. Kingston, JM: Island/Tuff Gong.

Massiah, L. (Producer & Director). (1997). *W. E. B. Du Bois: A biography in four voices.* Philadelphia: Scribe Video Center.

Mayfield, C. (1973). Future shock. On *Back to the world* [LP]. Chicago: Curtom Records.

McKissick, F. (1967/1969). Speech at the national conference on Black power. In Bosmajian, H. A. & Bosmajian, H. (Eds.), *The rhetoric of the civil-rights movement* (pp. 127–41). New York: Random House.

The meaning and measure of Black power. (1966, November). [Symposium]. *Negro Digest*, 20–37, 81–96.

Meistrich, L., Rotholz, R., Salerno, R., & Williams, H. (Producers), & Williams, H. (Director). (1998). *Belly*. New York: Artisan Entertainment.

Méliès, G. (Director). (1903). *A trip to Mars*. Paris, France: Star Film Company.

Meyer, R. (2016, July 21). Twitter's famous racist problem. *The Atlantic*. Retrieved from theatlantic.com

Mills, S. (2004). *Discourse*. 2nd edition. New York: Routledge.

Mitchell-Kernan, C. (1971). *Language behavior in a Black urban community*. Berkeley, CA: Language-Behavior Laboratory, University of California.

Mitchell-Kernan, C. (1972). Signifying, loud-talking and marking. In Kochman, T. (Ed.), *Rappin and stylin out: Communication in urban Black America* (pp. 315–35). Urbana, IL: University of Illinois Press.

Monte, E., Evans, M., Lear, N., Schwartz, E. (Writers), & Keith, G. (Director). (1977). Breaker, breaker. [Television series episode]. In Kalish, A., Kalish, I., Mitchell, G., Sunga, G., & Turner, L. (Producers). *Good times*. Los Angeles: Tandem Productions.

Morgan, J. (1999). *When chicken heads come home to roost: My life as a hip-hop feminist.* New York: Simon & Schuster.

Morrison, T. (1977). *Song of Solomon*. New York: Knopf.

Morrison, T. (1992). *Playing in the dark: Whiteness and the literary imagination*. Cambridge, MA: Harvard University Press.

Mortenson, E. (2010). *Capturing the beat moment: Cultural politics and the poetics of presence*. Carbondale, IL: Southern Illinois University Press.

Moses, W. J. (1975). The poetics of Ethiopianism. *American Literature*, 47, 411–26.

Moses, W. J. (1982). *Black Messiahs and Uncle Toms: Social and literary manipulations of a religious myth*. University Park, PA: Pennsylvania State University Press.

Mosley, W. (2008). *The right mistake: The further philosophical investigations of Socrates Fortlow*. New York: Basic Civitas.

Muhammad, E. (1973). *Message to the Blackman*. Phoenix: Secretarius MEMPS Publications.

Musgrave, M. (1971). Failing minority students: Class, caste, and racial bias in American colleges. *CCC*, 22(1), 24–9.

Neal, M. A. (2017, April 1). "If you don't own the [servers]": Curating + aggregating + doing Black digital studies in the digital era. *NewBlackMan (in exile)*. Retrieved from www.newblackmaninexile.net

The Negro will defend America. (1941). [Pamphlet]. Washington, DC: National Negro Congress.

Neill, R. W. (Director). (1923). *Mars calling*. USA.

Newman, R. (1998). Introduction. In Newman, R. (Ed.), *Go down, Moses: A celebration of the African-American spiritual* (pp. 18–27). New York: Clarkson/Potter.

Noble, S. U. (2018). *Algorithms of oppression: How search engines reinforce racism.* New York: New York University Press.

Nunley, V. (2011). *Keepin' it hushed: The barbershop and African American rhetoric.* Detroit: Wayne State University Press.

N. W. A. (1988). Dopeman. On *Straight Outta Compton* [LP]. Los Angeles: Ruthless Records.

Olney, James. (1985). "I was born": Slave narratives, their status as autobiography and as literature. In Davis, C. T. & Gates, H. L., Jr. (Eds.), *The slave's narrative* (pp. 148–75). New York: Oxford University Press.

Parler, N. (1958). Significant steps in successful language teaching: The communications approach. *CLA Journal, 2*(1), 42–50.

Parliament. (1975). *Mothership connection* [LP]. New York: Casablanca Records.

Patterson, L. T. (1936, April). Toward a brighter dawn. *The Woman Today, 14,* 30.

Perren, F., & St. Lewis, K. (1976). Heaven must be missing an angel [Recorded by Tavares]. On *Sky high!* [LP]. Los Angeles: Capitol Records.

Perton, M. (2016, October 14). Why doesn't anyone want to buy Twitter? *Newsweek.* Retrieved from newsweek.com

Plato. (2005a). Gorgias. (W. D. Woodhead, Trans.). In Hamilton, E. & Cairns, H. (Eds.), *Collected dialogues of Plato including the letters* (pp. 229–307). Princeton, NJ: Princeton University Press.

Plato. (2005b). Phaedrus. (R. Hackforth, Trans.). In Hamilton, E. & Cairns, H. (Eds.), *Collected dialogues of Plato including the letters* (pp. 475–525). Princeton, NJ: Princeton University Press.

Plato. (2005c). Republic. (P. Shorey, Trans.). In Hamilton, E. & Cairns, H. (Eds.), *Collected dialogues of Plato including the letters* (pp. 575–844). Princeton, NJ: Princeton University Press.

Porter, C. (1934). Anything goes [Recorded by Tony Bennett, 1955]. On *Strike up the band* [LP]. New York: Roulette.

Porter, C. (1934). Anything goes [Recorded by Ella Fitzgerald, 1956]. On *Ella Fitzgerald sings the Cole Porter songbook* [LP]. Los Angeles: Verve.

Porter, C. (1934). Anything goes [Recorded by Frank Sinatra, 1956]. On *Songs for swingin' lovers!* [LP]. Los Angeles: Capitol.

Pough, G. D. (2004). *Check it while I wreck it: Black womanhood, hip-hop culture, and the public sphere.* Boston: Northeastern University Press.

Pough, G. D. (2010). Greetings from the 2010 program chair. In *The remix: Revisit, rethink, revise, renew: CCCC 2010* (Conference Program, pp. 5–7). Urbana, IL: National Council of Teachers of English.

Powell, T. B., & Dobbs, C. (2017). Ebos landing. *New Georgia encyclopedia.* Retrieved from www.georgiaencyclopedia.org/articles/history-archaeology/ebos-landing

Pritchard, E. D. (2017). *Fashioning lives: Black queers and the politics of literacy.* Carbondale, IL: Southern Illinois University Press.

Putnam, A. (2012). *The insistent call: Rhetorical moments in Black anticolonialism, 1929–1937.* Amherst, MA: University of Massachusetts Press.

Queen Latifah. (1993). U.N.I.T.Y. On *Black reign* [CD]. Los Angeles: Motown.

Quintilian. (2015). *Institutes of oratory.* (J. S. Watson, Trans., C. Dozier & L. Honeycutt, Eds.). Printed version of John Selby Watson's translation of Quintilian's *Institutio oratoria.* Retrieved from http://rhetoric.eserver.org/

Ramsey, D. X. (2015, April 10). The truth about Black Twitter. *The Atlantic*. Retrieved from theatlantic.com

Ramsey, P. (1985). Teaching the teachers to teach Black-Dialect writers. In Brooks, C. (Ed.), *Tapping potential: English and language arts for the Black learner* (pp. 176–81). Urbana: IL: National Council of Teachers of English.

Reed, I. (1972/1976). *Mumbo jumbo*. New York: Avon.

Rich, A. (1972). When we dead awaken: Writing as re-vision. *College English*, 34(1), 18–30.

Richards, I. A. (1936). *The philosophy of rhetoric*. New York: Oxford University Press.

Richards, J. (2008). *Rhetoric*. London: Routledge.

Richardson, E. (2003). *African American literacies*. New York: Routledge.

Rojas, A. (2014). *Farrakhan asks President Obama to open Area 51 and reveal its UFO secrets*. Retrieved from www.huffingtonpost.com/alejandro-rojas/farrakhan-asks-president-_b_4850196.html

Romanski, A., Gardner, D., Kleiner, J. (Producers), & Jenkins, B. (Director). (2016). *Moonlight*. New York: A24 Films.

Rose, T. (1994). *Black noise: Rap music and Black culture in contemporary America*. Middletown, CT: Wesleyan University Press.

Royster, J. J. (1985). A new lease on writing. In Brooks, C. (Ed.), *Tapping potential: English and language arts for the Black learner* (pp. 159–67). Urbana, IL: National Council of Teachers of English.

Saussure, F. (1916/1966). *Course in general linguistics*. (W. Baskin, Trans.). New York: McGraw-Hill.

Savant, C. M. (2013). John Henry. On *Womanchild* [CD]. Grosse Pointe Farms, MI: Mack Avenue Records.

Sharma, S. (2013). Black twitter? Racial hashtags, networks and contagion. *New Formations: A Journal of Culture/Theory/Politics*, 78(1), 46–64.

Shirky, C. (2008). *Here comes everybody: The power of organizing without organizations*. New York: Penguin.

Sinclair, B. (2004). Integrating the histories of race and technology. In Sinclair, B. (Ed.), *Technology and the African-American experience: Needs and opportunities for study* (pp. 1–17). Cambridge, MA: The MIT Press.

Singleton, J. (Producer & Director). (2001). *Baby boy*. Los Angeles: Columbia Pictures.

Smitherman, G. (1977). *Talkin and testifyin: The language of Black America*. Boston: Houghton Mifflin.

Smitherman, G. (1979). Toward educational linguistics for the first world. *College English*, 41(2), 202–11.

Smitherman, G. (1994). "The blacker the berry, the sweeter the juice": African American student writers. In Dyson, A. H. & Genishi, C. (Eds.), *The need for story: Cultural diversity in classroom and community* (pp. 80–101). Urbana, IL: The National Council of Teachers of English.

Smitherman, G. (2000). "If I'm lyin, I'm flyin": The game of insult in Black Language. In *Talkin that talk: Language, culture, and education in African America* (pp. 223–30). New York: Routledge.

Smitherman, G. (2006). *Word from the mother: Language and African Americans*. New York: Routledge.

Solis, M. (2016, August 30). *Meet Moya Bailey, the black woman who created the term "misogynoir"*. Retrieved from M.mic.com

Southern, E. (1997). *The music of Black Americans: A history*. New York: W. W. Norton.

Steal away to Jesus. (2004). In Gilyard, K. & Wardi, A. (Eds.), *African American literature* (pp. 126–7). New York: Penguin Academics.

Stevie Wonder. (1972). *Talking book* [LP]. Los Angeles: Tamla Records.

Stevie Wonder. (2013). *Statement delivered by Stevie Wonder, United Nations Messenger of Peace, high-level meeting of the UN General Assembly on disability and development*. New York, 23 September 2013. Retrieved from www.un.org/en/ga/68/meetings/disability/pdf/wonder.pdf

Stewart, B. (1965). I do love you. On *I do love you* [LP]. Chicago: Chess Records.

Stewart, B. (1965). I do love you [Recorded by GQ, 1979]. On *Disco nights* [LP]. New York: Arista.

Stewart, M. (1833/2001). An address delivered at the African Masonic Hall, Boston, February 27, 1833. In Newman, R., Rael, P., & Lapsansky, P. (Eds.), *Pamphlets of protest: An anthology of early African American protest literature, 1790–1860* (pp. 123–7). New York: Routledge.

Stormont, L. (Director). (1909). *England invaded*. London, UK: Warwick Trading Company.

Stowe, H. B. (1852/1986). *Uncle Tom's cabin*. New York: Penguin Classics.

Sunjata. (1998). In Hill, P. L., Bell, B. W., Harris, W. J., Miller, R. B., O'Neale, S. A., & Porter, H. (Eds.), *The Riverside anthology of the African American literary tradition* (pp. 36–41). Boston: Houghton Mifflin.

Swing low, sweet chariot. (2004) In Gilyard, K. & Wardi, A. (Eds.), *African American literature* (p. 125). New York: Penguin Academics.

Toffler, A. (1970). *Future shock*. New York: Random House.

Tolentino, J. (2017, June 2). Sweet Jesus, Twitter CEO Jack Dorsey's #StayWoke shirt is incredibly embarrassing. *Jezebel*. Retrieved from jezebel.com

Truth, S. (1851/1998). Ar'n't I a woman? In Foner, P. S. & Branham, R. J. (Eds.), *Lift every voice: African American Oratory, 1787–1900* (pp. 226–9). Tuscaloosa, AL: The University of Alabama Press.

Turner, L. D. (1949). *Africanisms in the Gullah dialect*. Chicago: University of Chicago Press.

Van Evrie, J. H. (1868). *White supremacy and Negro subordination*.

Walker, A. (1973). Everyday use. In *In love & trouble: Stories of Black women*. Orlando, FL: Harvest.

Walker, A. (1974/1984). A letter to the editor of Ms. In *In search of our mothers' gardens* (pp. 273–7). San Diego: Harcourt Brace & Company.

Walker, A. (1984). *In search of our mothers' gardens*. San Diego: Harcourt Brace & Company.

Walker, A. (1989). A name is sometimes an ancestor saying hi, I'm with you. In *Living by the word* (pp. 97–8). San Diego: Harcourt Brace & Company.

Walker, D. (1829/1965). *An appeal to the coloured citizens of the world, but in particular, and very expressly, to those of the United States of America*. New York: Hill and Wang.

Walsh, R. (1819). *An appeal from the judgements of Great Britain respecting the United States of America*.

White, D. G. (1987). *Ar'n't I a woman?: Female slaves in the plantation south*. New York: W. W. Norton.

Whitehead, C. (2001). *John Henry days*. New York: Doubleday.

Whitfield, J. (1853/1998). America. In Hill, P. L., Bell, B. W., Harris, W. J., Miller, R. B., O'Neale, S. A., & Porter, H. (Eds.), *The Riverside anthology of the African American literary tradition* (pp. 377–81). Boston: Houghton Mifflin.

Wild Negro Bill. (1971). In Randall, D. (Ed.), *The Black poets* (p. 7). New York: Bantam.

Wilkerson, I. (2016). Where do we go from here? In Ward, J. (Ed.), *The fire this time: A new generation speaks about race* (pp. 59–61). New York: Scribner.

Wilkins, R. (1966/1969). Keynote address to the NAACP annual convention. In Bosmajian, H. A. & Bosmajian, H. (Eds.), *The rhetoric of the civil-rights movement* (pp. 89–100). New York: Random House.

Williams, S. (2015). Digital defense: Black feminists resist violence with hashtag activism. *Feminist Media Studies*, 15(2), 341–4.

Williamson, J. (1957). What can we do about it?: The contribution of linguistics to the teaching of English. *CLA Journal*, 1(1), 23–7.

Winthrop, J. (1630). A model of Christian charity.

Woodson, C. G. (1933/1990). The mis-education of the Negro. Trenton, NJ: Africa World Press.

Wright, R. (1940). *Native son*. New York: Harper & Brothers.

Young, R. A. (1829/2001). Ethiopian manifesto. In Newman, R., Rael, P., & Lapsansky, P. (Eds.), *Pamphlets of protest: An anthology of early African American protest literature, 1790–1860* (pp. 85–9). New York: Routledge.

Young, V. A. (2007). *Your average nigga: Performing race, literacy, and masculinity*. Detroit: Wayne State University Press.

Index

Note: Page numbers in *italic* indicate a figure on the corresponding page.

Made in the USA
Las Vegas, NV
01 March 2024

86568832R00085